Getting Jobs in
Broadcasting

CASSELL JOB GUIDES

Getting Jobs in Advertising
BY JENNY TIMBER

Getting Jobs in Beauty
BY LESLEY MOORE

Getting Jobs in Fashion Design
BY ASTRID A. KATCHARYAN

Getting Jobs in Graphic Design
BY TERRY JONES

Getting Jobs in Broadcasting
BY FIONA RUSSELL

Getting Jobs in Music
BY TONY ATTWOOD

Getting Jobs in Photography
BY KIM HOWARD

Getting Jobs in the Countryside
BY MURRAY MARSHALL

Getting Jobs in Broadcasting

Fiona Russell

CASSELL

Cassell Publishers Ltd
Artillery House, Artillery Row
London SW1P 1RT

First published 1989

British Library Cataloguing in Publication Data

Russell, Fiona
    Getting jobs in broadcasting. – (Cassell job guides)
    1. Great Britain. Broadcasting services. – Career guides
    I. Title
    384.54′ 023′ 41

ISBN 0–304–31702–0

Typeset by Chapterhouse, The Cloisters, Formby

Printed and bound in Great Britain by Biddles Ltd,
Guildford and King's Lynn

Contents

Who this book is for

This book is aimed at people who want to find out more about the career opportunities in film, video, television or radio.

Whether you are still at school considering subject options, at college looking at possible career paths, or even already in a job but considering a possible change, this book will give you relevant information about the broadcasting industry. It will help you to decide whether or not the industry is for you and, if so, to plan your next step.

There are a variety of routes into the industry; the difficulty is in deciding on the appropriate one for your particular background or what extra training or studies may be needed to enhance your opportunities. For example, there are some opportunities specifically for graduates, which will have accelerated training schemes. The companies which have graduate intakes are often listed in the normal graduate directories, available at college careers offices. Generally, however, the majority of paths available to the newcomer are through junior trainee posts and these are open to anyone who can demonstrate that they possess the appropriate skills. The more senior positions are recruited from within the companies themselves or from the industry as a whole.

This book covers all the main areas of work in film, video, television and radio. Each section gives some background information specific to that particular industry, the main job titles, responsibilities and requirements and provides profiles on some of the people working there. The book then goes on to look at what training courses exist and what qualifications are required, where additional training is available, advice on how to gain relevant experience, the entry routes and some practical steps to enhance your opportunities. A list of useful names and addresses of companies, organizations and educational institutions is given in Chapter 8.

The newcomer needs to be aware of what is ahead, to be able to recognize and optimize situations. The book will give a realistic picture of the competition. In this industry every job and training opportunity attracts a large response. You need to be single minded, highly motivated, have lots of energy, be willing to start at the bottom and not be put off if success doesn't happen immediately.

The key to success is getting a foot in the door – from there it is up to you to build up experience, make contacts, recognize opportunities and have the confidence to seize them.

The work is hard and it is not glamorous or star-studded. It requires people who show initiative, who can work in a team, who can work under pressure and who can meet deadlines.

This book will outline the skills and qualities you will need to break in, giving information on the jobs and hints on how to find them. Then, it is up to you to get involved, gain more experience and, with luck, get a foot in the door!

The industry explained

Broadcast and non-broadcast

Generally speaking, work in the industry is divided into two sectors, broadcast and non-broadcast. Broadcast refers to any production which is intended to be transmitted to the general public. This includes television and feature films. These productions are usually made by the better-known TV and film companies. The non-broadcast sector (also referred to as corporate production), is less well known, although there are many companies specializing in this work, producing tailor-made productions aimed at specific audiences rather than the general public. For example, a construction company might commission a production company to make a video or film about safety aspects on building sites, to be shown to new recruits. Safety issues, visually promoted on film or video, often have a greater impact than a site manager simply telling employees of the dangers. The subjects most frequently covered by the non-broadcast sector are in the areas of training, public relations, education and health and safety.

The technical and creative skills required by both the broadcast and non-broadcast sectors are very similar; the difference between them is in the equipment used. Broadcast standard demands highly sophisticated hardware which gives the picture quality seen on your television screen or at the cinema. This, and the commercial nature of this sector of the industry, tend to make the price of equipment phenomenal. Non-broadcast equipment, although less sophisticated, nevertheless requires detailed technical knowledge, so it is not necessarily any easier for the newcomer to find work in this sector than in public sector TV or film.

Companies in the non-broadcast sector aim to make their work as professional as their equipment will allow and they choose staff with a genuine interest in the industry and proven ability, often with broadcasting backgrounds.

Job titles and tasks vary depending on whether the production is made on film or video, for a television production, for a radio news programme or for a play. Some titles remain the same across all the media (e.g., producer, director, camera operator), and these people will, with a few differences, have similar responsibilities and skill requirements. In the following chapters we shall look at each of the areas of the media – film, video, television and radio – outlining job descriptions and explaining working practices.

The stages involved in making a production

The making of a production can be divided into three stages, with each stage requiring different jobs and skills. Some of the people, such as the producer or director, will be needed throughout the production, whilst others, such as the camera operator or editor, will only be needed at one particular stage.

The three stages are pre-production, production and post-production. The larger film, TV and radio companies may have the facilities to handle all three stages, but smaller companies usually complete only the first two stages themselves, then pass on the work of post-production to other companies.

Pre-production

This is probably the most important stage, because if ideas are not well thought out, planned and organized, the production may never get off the ground. The key tasks involved in the initial planning stages require a great deal of experience and an understanding of the production system as a whole. At this stage the plans have to be comprehensive, including estimates of how long the project will take, decisions about the kind of equipment required, crew to be hired, about locations to be booked, budget estimates and the necessary finance to be secured. The list goes on ... Few people just starting out in the industry will command a position of authority or influence within the pre-production stage. It demands professional ability, knowledge and experience.

The aim of pre-production is to get everything planned. For example, until everything is known about the requirements of the script, artists, crews, locations, studios, accommodation, transport, equipment hire and an estimate of how long the project is likely to take, the budget estimate for the production cannot be made. Until the total number of staff for production is known, transport, catering and accommodation cannot be planned. The demands of each project will differ depending on the pre-production schedule. The skills required for pre-production work will be the ability to organize, negotiate and represent the interests of the project.

Production

The work involved in this phase moves out from the office to location and studio work. At this stage most of the shooting and recording is done. Technicians and artists are brought together to work under the control of the director and producer. Because everyone must work closely with each other at this stage, good team work is required to

Stages in production

achieve the best results, therefore each technician must understand how his or her job relates to all the other job skills. Working hours can be long, depending on deadlines, and the whole crew must be able to work under pressure. Once the entire production has been shot, the work progresses to the next stage.

Post-production

When the production is in 'the can' or on tape, the final stage involves bringing the different strands of the production together to meet a professional standard. This post-production work varies, depending on what medium is used, and includes such work as editing and adding titles. There are many specialist organizations who offer specific post-production services to film, video, television and radio companies.

Traditional attitudes and values remain and many working practices are based solely on the attitude that 'it has always been done this way'. This is also true of the people who have traditionally been employed in certain jobs. Women and ethnic minorities are under-represented in many areas of work, although this situation is changing slowly. A greater awareness of equal opportunities within the industry is helping to promote access to these usually discriminated-against groups.

Many jobs in the industry are freelance so that a person is contracted for the duration of one project only. When the job is done, the contract ends. This method of employment has both advantages and disadvantages. It allows for more choice (probably more variety), but it does carry the risk of longer periods of unemployment, depending on what work is available.

Equal opportunities

To date, jobs in the broadcasting industry have been dominated by white males – the term cameraman should, more correctly, be camera person or operator. The majority of electricians, directors, producers and engineers are also male. Certain other jobs are predominantly female, for example, make-up artists, vision mixers and secretaries. People in the industry keen to encourage equal opportunities want to see a breakdown of the stereotypes and a better balance of the sexes in all jobs so that there will be equal opportunities for both men and women to pursue the jobs they want. Initiatives within the industry, for example the JOBFIT scheme and the technical training offered to women employees in some companies, are helping to change the situation.

Now that many companies are adopting equal opportunities policies, women and ethnic minorities in key jobs will increasingly provide newcomers with a positive role. This will help to break down traditional attitudes. However, it is important to remember that, irrespective of your sex, colour or background, you will need the appropriate skills in order to apply successfully for a job. Students contemplating a career in broadcasting should therefore take a good balance of subjects so as not to rule out any career area. Studying technical subjects as well as the arts and humanities is very important, as well as gaining experience with computers.

The future

In November 1988 the Government launched a White Paper titled *Broadcasting in the '90s: Competition, Choice and Quality*. It is a far-reaching document which looks into the future of broadcasting.

Opinions vary about exactly how technological changes will affect the media industry. Generally it is agreed that there will be massive changes in the 1990s. Some are calling this the 'broadcasting revolution'. Changes in Government policy, referred to as 'de-regulation', will also have profound effects on the monopoly of television and radio by the BBC, ITV companies and Independent Local Radio (ILR). Independent producers (not to be confused with the Independent Television companies), are negotiating to increase the number of productions they make for the BBC, ITV and ILR.

With the development of cable and satellite broadcasting, the choice of channels on offer will increase. The question which remains unanswered is whether or not the expansion in broadcasting will result in more jobs and improved prospects for newcomers. The general opinion is that there is unlikely to be a large increase in jobs connected to programme creation in either the technical or creative areas. However, expansion is likely to happen in sales and administration and, to a lesser extent, in the fields of electronic and communication engineering. Neither will the pathways into the industry, or job availability, radically change, so the competition will be as fierce as ever.

Having said this, working in the media industry is exciting, but if you really want to get in, you will have to work hard at building up your skills and learning to sell yourself.

2

The film industry

The film industry is fragmented, with numerous small companies each doing specific tasks which, together, make up the complete picture. Many of the organizations are based in London but in most cities several companies involved in film making can be found.

Traditionally, only the large studios made films. Names like Pinewood and Shepperton spring to mind. Nowadays these studios no longer make films. Instead they provide a facility, by hiring out their floor space to production companies, and so they are often now referred to as 'four-wallers'. Production crews go to the studio, set up their equipment, shoot the film and leave when the job is completed.

Only a few organizations in the film industry are household names. This makes it harder for the newcomer to find out who and where the companies are and, more importantly, how to approach them. An easy way to familiarize yourself with some names would be to consult trade directories or, when you next go to a cinema, make a note of the film companies shown in the credits.

As previously mentioned, there are basically three stages in the making of a film: pre-production, production and post-production. For each stage, there are numerous specialist companies which provide services and equipment. The variety of these is vast, for example lighting equipment hire, studio space, cutting rooms, sound dubbing, animation, optical effects and titles. Hence the number of companies involved in each project is vast, as the film is passed from one specialist company to the next, rather like an assembly line, until the project is completed. It is the special job of what is called a production company to co-ordinate the whole project from pre-production through production to its completion in post-production, and finally pass it on to the distributor whose job is to sell it.

Film format and equipment

Much of the equipment used in the film industry is still very traditional. Cameras and editing equipment which were of robust construction are still much in evidence today. New technology has enhanced film techniques but not changed them radically, although some advances have made components smaller and equipment lighter. For this reason some equipment is now easier to use. The size and format of the film used varies according to what it is to be used for. Most feature films are made on 16-mm or 35-mm film. Some more recent productions (like *Star Trek 3*) use 70-mm film. The larger the film the better the resolution and clarity. Other advances have been the use of even larger screens, stereo sound and Dolby noise reduction.

What do production companies make films about?

Feature films

Because film production in Britain is sporadic it is hard to predict from one year to the next how many feature films are likely to be made. Feature films are costly to produce and so a production company has to be sure of success at the box office before financial backers will invest in the project. Many recent British low-budget films (still relatively expensive) like *Letter to Brezhnev* and *My Beautiful Laundrette* have been very successful, which helps British companies to stay in existence. In addition to those films which are made for a mass audience, films are also deliberately made for smaller audiences. These films, made by enthusiasts in film and video workshops, are often produced on unbelievably low budgets.

Commercials

Organizations wishing to promote products spend a great deal of money on advertising. There is no better way of getting a message across to a lot of people than through television. Many production companies specialize in making adverts to be shown on television and in the cinema. Generally, more money is spent per second producing a commercial than a feature film. This is because all the stages of production will still be needed even though the finished commercial is very much shorter than the average feature film. The average length of an advert on TV is 30 seconds, while the average film lasts 90 minutes, and yet the advertising images and characters are often strong and memorable. Thus, the advertising industry also requires highly skilled and professional staff.

Documentaries

Some film makers only work on documentaries, as they enjoy the challenge of working on current issues, natural history and world events.

Training films

Today, in industry and business, training materials have become an essential feature. Films are made on every type of training you can imagine, from selling techniques to information for new recruits and management skills. Some training films are designed for all employees, while others are more specific (e.g., shown only to a particular department). Some film companies specialize in making only training films.

Health and safety films

Many organizations which promote awareness about health and safety, such as the Health Education Council, often commission films outlining some particular aspect of danger. These films are aimed at promoting public awareness. Here again the potential audience may be large, and the films may cover a variety of topics. Drugs, alcohol abuse and smoking have been the subject of many such films. Other films may have a more specifically targeted audience, for example, a petrochemical company may want a film which explains the various hazards of fire and chemicals to its on-site employees.

Public relations films

Recognizing the power of the broadcasting media, many companies now use films to promote good public relations. These films differ from straight commercials in that they generally promote an image of the company as a whole, rather than any of its particular products. The aim of such films is to make their audience more aware of the corporate identity of a company. For example, an Electricity Board film may focus

attention on how electricity affects our lives. It does not, in itself, seek to persuade us to use more electricity. It merely aims to give us a better understanding of what the Electricity Board does. Another example of this type of public relations use of film is a film commissioned by a multi-national company showing how profitable the company is and outlining its achievements. Such films are often made to be shown at the annual general meeting of shareholders, or to promote the company's services to prospective customers.

Key jobs in the film industry explained

Camera crew

Cinematographer

The cinematographer is responsible for lighting and camera angles. Experience will show what camera position would be best under particular lighting conditions. This is important in the changeable British climate. If the director requires a particular mood the cinematographer must be able to capture it whether the scene is shot in natural morning or afternoon sunlight. If the weather is dull, lights could enhance the picture. The cinematographer's experience will also allow the right choice of lenses and filters to be made to create the mood the director is looking for.

Camera operator

The camera operator controls the camera and sees the shots the director and the cinematographer want. Good communication skills, the ability to follow instructions, an eye for detail and a patient attitude are required for this position within the crew.

Focus puller

The focus puller ensures the correct lens is on the appropriate camera and that the distance between the subject and the camera is correct to get the shot in focus. Lenses are expensive and must be carefully stored to avoid damage and the focus puller is responsible for their care. A technical understanding of the equipment is essential.

Camera grip (key grip/dolly grip)

The camera grip is responsible for moving the camera, checking that it is secured and, when used for tracking shots, can easily be pushed.

Clapper loader

The clapper loader is responsible for loading film in the cameras and ensuring there is enough film for each take. The clapper loader keeps notes for each camera on the type of film used, what lenses have been used and, of course, snaps the clapper board on the command of 'action'. This identifies each piece of film shot and will assist the editor later on.

Continuity

SCRIPT SUPERVISOR

The script supervisor is responsible for script continuity throughout filming, making sure that everything is correct between scenes or from one day to the next. This ensures that the script details have been followed. Continuity notes are kept on each shot, as filming is not always shot in sequence. An eye for detail and a good memory are essential so that faults can be spotted and corrected prior to filming. Polaroid photographs help to keep accurate logs.

Design

ART DIRECTOR

The art director is concerned with the design of the production and creating sets which are convincing. Many art directors have started their careers by studying design subjects at college, such as graphics or interior design.

SET DRESSER

The set dresser works to the art director's instructions. After the set has been constructed and painted, the set dresser then adds furniture and the interiors. An appreciation of textiles and interiors helps the dresser to interpret the art director's instructions.

PROPS BUYER

The props buyer is responsible for supplying props for the set, which can either be bought or hired. These can be anything from farm machinery and animals to jewellery.

MAKE-UP ARTIST

Make-up includes hairdressing and make-up as well as creating special effects such as scars. The make-up artist must be able to work with actors and be able to translate the brief from the art director and director. Early morning starts are frequent before filming begins for the day.

WARDROBE

The wardrobe assistant keeps costumes cleaned and well maintained. This job involves a lot of ironing, washing and mending.

Direction

DIRECTOR

The director is in charge of the creative aspects of the film and is responsible for both actors and the camera shots. It takes many years learning the skills of the film business before one achieves the position of director. The director has to be good at communicating ideas. The director will guide the actors through the script and work through the crew's plans. The director must also have technical understanding of the film equipment. At the end of a day's filming, 'rushes' are viewed in a preview theatre to ensure the image produced is giving the desired effect. The director spends time with the editor in cutting rooms, checking that the editing produces the right pictures.

FIRST, SECOND, THIRD ASSISTANT DIRECTORS

The three assistant directors work under the director and are involved in the day-to-day organization. They each have responsibilities to keep the production running as smoothly as possible.

Editing

EDITOR

After the shooting is complete and the film has been processed, the editor cuts and joins the film to produce the final product. The editor will work with location notes and a script and a brief to make the film flow so that it holds the audience's attention. A good working relationship with the director will make the job easier. Editors need an eye for detail and a lot of patience; the work can take many weeks in small, dimly lit cutting rooms.

ASSISTANT EDITOR

The assistant editor keeps careful record of what shots have been included and which have been cut out. All film which has been cut out at the editing stage is kept in case there is a change of mind. Nothing is thrown away.

Electricians

GAFFER

The gaffer is the supervising electrician responsible for lighting, who will advise the cinematographer on lighting effects.

BEST BOY

The best boy is the second electrician, working under the gaffer.

Opticals

ROSTRUM CAMERA OPERATOR

Anything that cannot be done in live action can be achieved on a rostrum camera. It is used for superimposing animation, titles or effects. (In the case of cartoons, it is used for filming animation.) The rostrum camera is vertically mounted, and animated work is superimposed on a projection of the live action. The complete section is refilmed, one frame at a time, and after processing the end result looks 'real'.

Production

PRODUCER

The producer is responsible for the finance, organization and administration of the production. The producer must be a methodical worker, able to keep a number of projects running smoothly simultaneously and able to think ahead. The producer obtains the script, estimates the budget, secures funding for the production, selects locations and hires crew. The ability to plan how long the production will take and to keep to the timetable so that the production does not go over budget requires a lot of experience.

PRODUCTION ASSISTANT (PA)

The PA is responsible for the administrative backup to the producer. This is a very demanding job requiring good secretarial skills, the ability to think ahead, keep track of deadlines, keep calm in a crisis, deal with several problems at once and have good reserves of energy. The demands made on the PA will depend on the size of the production and duties can include organizing accommodation and transport, typing script changes, liaising between the producer and other members of the crew and keeping administrative work up to date and organized. Many PAs start as production secretaries, the major difference being that the secretary, unlike the PA, is based at the production office not on location.

PRODUCTION MANAGER

The production manager is concerned with the day-to-day running of the production and works under the producer. The production manager oversees the finances and is responsible for the production being completed within the budget. If filming is to be done in the centre of a city, the production manager is responsible for notifying the appropriate authorities and gaining permission. On large productions there will be a location manager to assist the production manager.

RUNNER

The runner or 'gofer' (pronounced 'go fur', as in 'go for this/that') is the person who has a wide range of responsibilities which can be classified as 'all the junior tasks no one else has time to do'. Working on location is demanding; hours are long and tempers fragile. A runner's day starts early and involves making endless cups of tea for the crew as well as running errands. A driving licence is an advantage; if something is urgently required the runner may have to go to the nearest town to buy it. A runner needs an outgoing personality, the ability to work in a team and under pressure, and a thick skin.

Preview/rushes theatre

PROJECTIONIST

A preview or rushes theatre is a small, privately owned cinema usually seating ten to a hundred people. On a major production, the film will be processed and viewed each evening by the director and other crew members to ensure that lighting and camera angles are giving the desired effect. The projectionist is responsible for lacing up the film and care has to be taken when handling the film so as not to damage it. While the film is running the projectionist makes sure that the equipment is working smoothly and will set up the next reel of film to carry on from the last. The preview theatre is also used to show completed productions to film critics prior to the première.

Sound

BOOM OPERATOR

The boom operator is probably an ideal job for someone interested in both sound recording and fishing! The microphone is attached to a 'fish-pole' (or boom) which is very like a fishing rod. The position of the boom is determined by the sound mixer and must be out of camera view, but close enough to pick up the required sound. When this is not possible, radio microphones are attached to the actors' clothing. The boom operator will specialize in either location or studio work.

SOUND MIXER

The sound mixer records live sound, balancing levels and equalization on portable sound tape recorders. Some sound mixers work in the studio, mixing dialogue, music and special effects.

DUBBING MIXER

The dubbing mixer works in a specialized sound post-production studio. He or she must mix the final sound track onto the film, incorporating dialogue, music and special effects. Additional material may be required, which can be obtained from sound tape libraries which have pre-recorded master tapes of every sound imaginable. These can be mixed in to enhance the existing sound.

Profile

Film projectionist – Samantha

Sam has been working as a film projectionist for a year: here is her story so far . . .

Sam took a good mix of O levels and passed English language and literature, maths, geography, German and biology. Unfortunately, she did not pass physics, but her studies did enable her to feel confident about the basic principles of the subject. Sam was not keen to go on to A levels and wanted to do something practical which could help her to get into television. She was interested in camera work but was not sure how to get into the industry.

Sam secured a place on a BTEC National Diploma course in engineering at her local further education college. The course included electronics and telecommunications. There were 30 students on the course — two were female! Sam said it was important to prove you were genuinely interested and able to cope with the technical aspects of the course. Only after that did the males respect you. Technically the course was demanding, Sam says the only technical thing she had done prior to the course was to take radios apart and make a futile attempt at cutting and splicing audio tape. Towards the end of the two-year course Sam applied to the BBC for a camera operator's post. She got as far as the third interview but failed, which was a great disappointment.

Sam wrote speculative letters to film companies asking for junior jobs and she kept in touch with her careers office. At the same time, she took a job working in a shop to earn some money. Although this was not what she wanted to do, it was useful experience as it gave her the confidence to talk to people she did not know. Sam took a week's holiday and, on her return, followed up all the leads and contacts she could. Her efforts paid off and she got a job in a small preview theatre as a trainee projectionist.

Her first impressions of the industry were that everyone seemed to know everyone else and she did not know anyone. The technical side of the work was very daunting. Sam vividly remembers lacing up a projector for the first time and being very nervous. The owner and head projectionist gave Sam film to practise on which helped her to become quicker and more confident. After a film has been shown, it has to be rewound, and this was another task Sam took on. It helped her to appreciate how to handle film, that it is easily scratched or torn and that a lot of care must be taken.

In addition to learning the technical side, Sam was also involved in answering the 'phone, taking bookings, greeting clients, making coffee and keeping the theatre tidy. Preview theatres are often used to preview a new production for critics and refreshments are usually provided. After Sam has run a film, a buffet lunch may be served and she helps out by pouring drinks. While doing all this, she is often very aware that other clients have been booked in for the next preview. Meanwhile, no one seems to be in a particular hurry to leave and the place has to be tidied before the next client arrives. As a result, there is often an overlap and she also has to look after clients who have just arrived.

Sam feels it is very important to have a good memory for names and faces, as she will often deal with the same clients. She frequently does the first booking of the day, and has to leave home at 5.30 a.m. to get to work on time. The owner tends to do the late night bookings. The working day can be very long, but when someone 'phones with a booking you must always sound enthusiastic, even when you know it means you will be staying late. Sam often works at weekends.

Sam's main leisure activity is going to the cinema, so working in a preview theatre is ideal for her. When a production company is doing a feature film, they may book the theatre each evening for a couple of months. As a projectionist, you see the rushes and can see how the editor skilfully cuts the film down from eleven cans to nine, six or five and the final product emerges. Sam says it is very important to keep calm under pressure, no matter what happens. Keeping a cool head will enable you to sort out a problem logically.

Sam is keen to advance within the film industry and is interested in editing work. Her experience has given her a feel for what people do in the industry and how a production fits together. She is now waiting for the right opportunity to come along; when it does she will take it.

3
The video industry

Video tape was first used in the late 1950s. Since then there has been a dramatic expansion in the use of this medium. The major factor which separates video tape from film is its immediacy, as it does not need to be processed in a laboratory. Once shot, the video cassette can be played on a compatible video cassette recorder (VCR). Video tape is cheaper than film stock and is therefore popular with groups and organizations operating on low budgets. Having said that tape is cheaper, however, the final cost of a video production may not differ much from the cost of a film especially if sophisticated computer graphics are used for titles and animation.

Despite advances in video technology and the range of equipment available, the video medium is still not considered as creative as film. At present, film camera optics still have the edge on video for a creative production, as the definition and clarity of film is better. The situation is further complicated by having three different video standards, which are PAL, NTSC and SECAM. For example, the USA, Japan and Canada use the NTSC standard. The UK and most of Europe use the PAL standard, and France and the USSR use SECAM. Since these standards are not compatible with each other, so-called 'facility houses' have been established to specialize in standards' conversion and duplication (or copying). If, for example, a production company makes a video for worldwide distribution, it will have to take into account the differing standards in each country. It will pass the video to one of these facility houses to convert it to the relevant standard. It could be argued that having three standards has not speeded the development of this medium. Not surprisingly, therefore, technicians in the industry choose film for many projects, especially for feature films or productions where artistic photography is important. For other productions, video is the natural choice due to its flexibility, convenience and cost effectiveness.

As in the film industry, there are many companies, also known as 'facility houses', who offer a particular video service, for example hire of equipment, studio and editing facilities. Few organizations could afford to buy all the equipment that is required to make a production. Hiring equipment enables a production company to keep production costs down and gives it a wider choice.

Again, as with film, video production companies are often small, employing only a few staff. When working on a production, companies hire freelance crews to make the video. Video post-production companies generally employ more staff, such as trained technicians involved in editing, duplication and transfer and computer graphics.

Many large organizations (referred to as the corporate sector), such as banks and manufacturing companies, have 'in-house' video production units. Some of these may have the means to make productions totally in-house, while others will use outside facilities houses for some of the production work. When companies need extra personnel for productions, freelance crews can be hired for the duration of the production.

What is video used for?

Training and education

Video is ideal for situations where instant playback is required. For example, when training in interview techniques, people taking part in role play can see on a television monitor exactly how they have performed. This makes coaching and counselling easier. Also, the video tape can either be given to the trainees for later reference or re-used. Many videos are made as teaching aids for induction training for new staff.

News gathering

Television companies' news crews use video to record up-to-the-minute reports on current events. Electronic News Gathering (ENG) camera crews are sent out to record information, after which the crew return to the studio, edit the tape, add the commentary and the pictures are seen on the television news that evening.

Corporate production

Increasingly, companies not involved in the video industry use it in promotion, public relations, marketing and training. A video will promote a product, for example a food processor. A department store can run a video on a continuous loop, showing customers the features of the food processor, in an attempt to generate sales for the product. Corporate videos are in the non-broadcast sector.

Pop promos

The music industry has encouraged the expansion of video production. All the major record companies produce not only the record, music cassette and compact disc, but also a video to promote the music, the band and their image. In some cases, pop videos have played a greater part in the success of the record than the song itself.

Pre-recorded videos

Approximately 50 per cent of UK households have a video cassette recorder. The sales of pre-recorded video cassettes, particularly of movies, has expanded, posing a real threat to cinema audience attendance.

Video publishing

This is another area of expansion. Traditionally, consumers would buy a book on a particular subject. Now it is possible to buy a video instead of, or as a supplement to, a book, to receive information on anything from keep fit to cookery.

Video conferencing

Usually broadcasting and telecommunication companies buy the majority of satellite time. With the increasing availability of satellite 'slots', it is now possible for more companies to link up their audiences in different parts of the country (or globe) simultaneously. This has led to the development of 'video conferencing', where, for example, a multi-national company based in the UK can hold a two-way conference between its head office and all its subsidiary companies around the world. As awareness of the potential of satellites grows, more companies will probably use video conferencing as a means of communication.

Video equipment is high tech, sophisticated, state-of-the-art technology. The technicians who maintain the equipment need a good understanding of electronics and electrical principles. The majority would have had formal training. The technicians who operate the equipment, while not needing such in-depth knowledge, do still need technical competence.

Key jobs in the video industry explained

Camera

Camera operator

The camera operator is responsible for taking the shots to the requirements of the director, using the appropriate lenses and filters. The operator needs a good technical understanding of the equipment's potential. Experience of amateur and/or college productions will provide a basic understanding of this area of work. The camera operator has a key job in a production and employers look for some kind of previous experience.

Camera assistant

The camera assistant helps the operator; duties include helping to carry and set up the equipment. It is also the assistant's responsibility to keep lenses stored ready for use. Other duties are likely to include checking and cataloguing tape stocks for each shoot. It is vital that the assistant participates as a member of the team and responds to the instructions of the operator.

Direction

Director

The director is in control of the creative and artistic direction of the production. The director translates the script visually, making creative decisions which interpret the ideas. The director needs to have a technical understanding and an ability to communicate instructions

clearly to both the technical crew and the actors. The director also works with the editor in post-production, ensuring that the final edit is what was envisaged when shooting began. To assist in this process, regular progress review meetings are held with the production team. One advantage of video is that the day's shoot can easily be viewed.

Editing

Editor

The video process is unlike film in that the video tape is not cut. The original tape (the master) is copied and the editor works on this, copying the desired sequence onto a blank cassette in another machine. The editor works to the script with the director, assembling pictures and sound to create a smooth flowing production. The video editor's skill lies in keyboard dexterity and a good technical understanding of the equipment.

Assistant video editor

The assistant ensures that there is enough blank tape stock for the editor, checks the script and location notes, and keeps a record of what cuts the editor is making. The assistant liaises with clients, often explaining what the editor is doing and what result will be produced. The assistant must have an eye for detail and be quick to learn.

Electrician

The electrician is in charge of wiring and setting up the lights. The electrician needs a good grasp of electrics and most lighting electricians will have studied for City and Guilds qualifications at a further education college. Work varies, depending on whether the job is in a studio or on location. In a studio there is a lighting grid from which lights are hung. On location, lighting is supported on portable stands. The lighting electrician sets up the lighting according to a plan.

Graphics designer

The graphics designer prepares artwork for titles and captions. These are added in post-production and most of the work is done on a computer.

Production

Producer

The producer organizes the production and oversees the budgets. The producer needs to be aware of all aspects of the work and also needs to know what creative skills and what equipment are required to interpret the script to the client's wishes.

Production assistant

The production assistant is the back-up person working with the director, producer and production manager. The production assistant is involved, from the beginning to the end of the production, in technical aspects as well as in administration. The production assistant needs to be highly organized, have a good working knowledge of the industry, and be able to think ahead and consider a multitude of potential problems. Typing and keyboard skills are essential.

Production manager

The production manager organizes and co-ordinates the job and works under the producer. The production manager is responsible for a wide range of tasks, from pre-production through to the completion of shooting. The production manager works closely with the producer and has to be aware of the budget limitations and time schedules. He or she will hire equipment, book catering services, organize locations and troubleshoot to avoid any problems which may delay the production. The production manager must be technically competent and be aware of the range of equipment that can be hired and its availability. He or she will also hire crews and draw up contracts.

Runner

The runner (also called the 'gofer' or messenger) is a junior job and this post is the way in for most newcomers to the industry. The runner's responsibilities are basically doing anything and everything no one else has the time or energy to do. Duties vary depending on whether the job is in production or post-production.

Many newcomers to the industry will start as runners in post-production because facility houses tend to employ a runner as a full-time employee rather than on a freelance basis. Starting in post-production gives the newcomer insight into the industry and the opportunity to learn skills and make decisions about the next move. Work can involve many duties, some very basic, others carrying more responsibility. Either way, the runner must do everything efficiently and effec-

tively. Work can involve a lot of delivery and collection duties, such as taking video cassettes to other clients or facility houses, and collecting them later. A driving licence is useful.

Sound engineer

The sound engineer's job varies depending on whether he or she is working on production or post-production. On location (production), the sound engineer is responsible for recording the sound onto a portable tape recorder. This will include setting up microphones, checking sound levels and balance. In the studio, the sound engineer can then mix the live recording with voice-overs or sound effects. Some sound effects, for example a thunderclap or a car screeching to a halt, may not be possible to record on location. Sound effect libraries have every sound you can imagine and they can be mixed in to enhance the sound track. Music may also be added at this stage for extra effect. Some productions are shot without any sound, in which case the sound track is added in at the post-production stage. This is particularly common in commercials.

Video engineer

The video engineer is concerned with ensuring that both the video cameras and video tape recorders (VTR) are correctly linked. The picture is monitored to ensure a clear recording. When more than one video camera is being used, it is important to set each camera so that it produces the same quality of picture in terms of colour, contrast and brightness. This will avoid possible problems during the editing stage, when the results from each camera are combined. The engineer is also responsible for the maintenance of equipment and for sorting out technical problems. The engineer can work either on location or in a facility house.

Video operator

The video operator is generally employed in post-production and is involved in checking the technical equipment to ensure the picture quality is up to standard. Facility houses which are involved in editing, duplicating and tele-cine transfer employ operators.

Profile

Assistant video editor – Sally

Sally has been with the same video post-production company since leaving school. She started as a runner but quickly progressed to the position of assistant video editor where she is learning the skills of editing.

When Sally was at school she had no particular career ideas except that she knew she did not want to work in a shop or an office. She was interested in the theatre, television and magazines, but was not sure what jobs were open to the newcomer. Sally went on to study A levels which gave her more time to make career decisions. Meanwhile, in her summer holidays, Sally did a course on video and television. This gave her the opportunity to get 'hands on' experience in the studio and helped her to make up her mind about what she wanted to do when she left school. Sally studied A levels in art, sociology and theatre studies; she had no plans to go on to higher education. Instead, she decided to find a job after her exams. Unfortunately, Sally failed her A levels, but re-took and passed art and sociology.

Sally got in touch with her careers office which gave her advice on speculative applications and job interviews. She took a lot of time over her curriculum vitae (CV) which set out clearly her qualifications and her work experience, including the training in film and video. She sent out many speculative applications and she also called personally on companies and left her CV. She found that companies were generally quite happy to recommend other firms who had vacancies. Many of the jobs she went for had already been filled or required a driving licence. Others said they wanted a boy because there was heavy lifting (despite the fact that this objection contravened the sex discrimination law).

Sally was eventually taken on as a runner by a company involved in film and video editing. Her job involved a lot of delivery work taking videos or films to other companies or collecting film from laboratories. One of the worst aspects of being a runner is being at everyone's beck and call. Everyone thinks their job is the most urgent and the junior person finds it impossible to decide which job should be done first. There was a lot of making cups of tea and coffee and running errands (mopping the kitchen floor was one of the less interesting jobs). The hardest job was doing delivery work in the snow.

Sally got on well and after seven months of being the runner she was promoted to become an assistant video editor. Sally feels the assistant has got to be 'one step ahead' and be able to listen to two conversations at once to get a feel of what the clients are wanting, while also being aware of what the video editor is doing, as well as making sure there are enough tapes, etc.

Sally's plans for the future are to gain as much experience in editing as possible, including learning how to operate the low-band video editing equipment. The most difficult aspect is having the confidence in your own creative skills, knowing where to edit and working under a lot of pressure.

Sally does have an interest in getting into production work on commercials. She is curious to see what happens to the commercial before it arrives at the video editing suite for post-production.

4
Television

Television companies are household names ... or are they? Certainly the four main organizations, BBC1, BBC2, ITV and Channel 4 are well known. However, many programmes on broadcast television are made by relatively unknown companies. These companies make up the 'independent sector' and, like the main organizations, are potential employers, so newcomers should be aware of their importance. The development of these emerging companies has been enhanced by the 'television revolution' which has allowed them increased access to the network. The advent of cable and satellite will no doubt have repercussions on many companies within the independent sector.

Notable dates

The BBC began the first public television service in 1936 and Independent Television started up in 1955. BBC2 was introduced in 1964 and a little later colour television arrived. The second independent channel, Channel 4, and the Welsh Channel, Sianel Pedwar Cymru (S4C – the Welsh fourth channel), began broadcasting in 1982.

The 1990s hold more changes as technology advances, such as high definition television which offers a better quality picture.

British Broadcasting Corporation (BBC)

The BBC is a huge corporation, organized into different regions, producing programmes for BBC1 and BBC2, the majority of which are transmitted nationally. They also produce a few regional programmes which are broadcast locally. The bulk of the corporation's output is made in-house by the BBC. Some programmes are bought from overseas or made for the BBC by the independent sector. The many different BBC departments include: Light Entertainment, Documentary Features, Music and Arts, TV News, Schools Broadcasting, TV Plays, Science and Features, Children's Programmes, Current Affairs, the Community Programme Unit and Religious Programmes. Each department operates somewhat like a separate company, although each is held accountable to the Director General. BBC Enterprises is responsible for selling videos, books and merchandise related to the corporation's programmes. BBC Enterprises also markets the programmes to television companies abroad.

BBC training

The BBC regularly recruits trainees to specific areas and competition for the limited number of places is fierce. Training schemes are open to school and college leavers from the age of eighteen plus and usually require a minimum of good GCSE passes and A levels, or equivalent.

Trainees are taken on in the following areas:

Secretarial and clerical

Annually the BBC advertises for secretarial and clerical trainees. It offers office training courses, especially the Trainee Teeline Course and the Typing and Office Duties Course. The minimum requirement for these courses are A levels. No previous typing or shorthand experience is necessary. On completion of the course, trainees are attached to a department and continue their training before being placed in permanent posts.

Engineering and technical operations

The BBC regularly recruits technical operators, trainee engineers and engineers for specialized training. The minimum age is eighteen. Normal hearing and colour vision are essential. The minimum qualifications required for technical operators are GCSE passes in maths, English and physics. Trainee engineers require GCSE passes in maths, English and physics, and to have studied maths and physics to A-level standard or the equivalent BTEC National Diploma in electrical/electronic engineering. To join as an operational engineer a degree or HND (with merit passes in four H-level subjects including maths) is required in electrical/electronic engineering, applied physics, or a similar subject. Trainee Engineers (Graduates) is an annual scheme aimed at recruiting graduates not qualified as engineers who wish to transfer into broadcast engineering. In addition to the qualifications required for each of these posts, the BBC is looking for applicants who have relevant interests and hobbies over and above their educational ones: for example, photography, music, hospital or amateur radio, electronics or running a disco. Applicants must be able to work in a team, work under pressure, meet deadlines and be willing to work unsocial hours.

Film

Occasionally the BBC recruits film trainees for assistant posts in camera work, sound recording, editing and projection. The minimum age is eighteen and applicants should have a good general education including English and maths (or physics). It is important that candidates have demonstrable practical experience and skills. Applicants must therefore have an active interest in film and film making, a strong interest in photography and the cinema and have had practical experience of handling film and video. Normal colour vision and hearing are required.

Make-up

The BBC recruits and trains make-up assistants. The minimum age required is twenty and a half, and applicants should have a good educational background, preferably to A-level standard. Proven interest in make-up for television, theatre or film, as well as practical training in hairdressing or art are required. Make-up assistants work in television studios as well as on location, in all weather conditions, and the hours can be long and unpredictable. Applicants must be able to demonstrate their artistic flair and have a pleasant personality. The latter is important. Make-up assistants must be tactful and sympathetic towards all types of people. Normal colour vision is required.

Training schemes for graduates (non-engineering)

Available schemes include training for:

Television production trainees
Radio production trainees
World Service production trainees
News trainees

Trainee studio managers
Local radio trainee reporters
  (see p. 64)
Personnel trainee scheme

These training schemes are very popular. Whilst they are not exclusively aimed at graduates, many applicants have studied higher education courses. The BBC is looking for people who can demonstrate real enthusiasm for broadcasting. The BBC does not specify particular subjects, but is looking for applicants with a creative and original mind and the ability to criticize constructively and to turn ideas into programmes. The standard of the successful applicants is very high, and many would have had practical involvement in broadcasting or journalism in clubs or societies during their time at college, as well as a wide interest in current affairs and the media.

Sponsorships: engineering and technical operations

Each year, a small number of sponsorships (in the form of a bursary to supplement a grant) are awarded to students embarking on degree courses in:

Specializations	Degrees
Research	Honours degree in electronic engineering
Designs	Honours degree in electronic engineering

Specializations	Degrees
Television operations	Degree in electronic engineering at university/polytechnic
Radio operations	Degree in electronic engineering at university/polytechnic
Transmitter projects	Honours degree in electronic engineering

Applications are welcomed from students in the final year of A-level study and from students established on the courses above.

Independent Broadcasting Authority (IBA)

The IBA is the public body authorized by Parliament to organize and supervise the independent broadcasting system. The system comprises a network of transmitters from which the independent broadcasting companies broadcast their programmes nationally. The companies using the network include the ITV companies, Independent Local Radio (ILR) and Britain's first direct broadcast satellite (DBS) contract was operated by Sky; British Satellite Broadcasting (BSB) is scheduled to come on air by spring 1990.

The IBA also regulates independent TV and radio and all the companies involved pay rental to the IBA to cover its cost in administrating the systems and operating its network of transmitters.

Channel 4, however, is arranged differently. It is regulated by the IBA but, unlike the ITV companies (which are franchised), it is a wholly owned subsidiary of the IBA. The ITV companies meet the costs of Channel 4 through separate subscription.

In the White Paper on broadcasting the Government does not believe the present system provided by the IBA should be continued. The Independent Television Commission (ITC) will look at the television system as a whole to ensure that the various enterprises are able to compete on equal terms and standards are maintained. The ITC will replace both the Cable Authority and the IBA.

Independent Television companies (ITV)

Independent Television is operated on a regional network basis. The United Kingdom is divided up into fourteen ITV areas. (London, uniquely, has two companies, one operating on weekdays, the other taking over for Friday evening and the weekend.) With the inclusion of TV-am, there is a total of sixteen ITV companies, and all are franchised by the IBA. Some programmes made by each ITV company are regional programmes with local interest. These are often broadcast during the day. At other times, all the regional ITV companies unite to broadcast nationally. Most of the programmes on ITV are made by the individual members for the network. Central, Granada, LWT, Thames and Yorkshire make the majority of these programmes for ITV and these companies are often referred to as the 'majors'. As with the BBC, some programmes are bought in from abroad.

ITV companies are funded by television advertising. Advertising agencies spend large sums of money on behalf of their clients to advertise products to the viewing public. It is this money which funds programme making.

TV-am provides early morning programming for all the ITV regions.

Independent Television News (ITN) covers all news programmes for ITV and Channel 4.

Channel 4 differs from all the other companies in that it does not produce any programmes itself (except *Right to Reply*, which allows viewers to comment on current programmes shown). Channel 4 purchases programmes, series and films from the independent sector in the UK and abroad, as well as from the ITV companies. In Channel 4's programme policy, the objectives were set out to cater specifically for tastes and interests not served, or under-represented, elsewhere on TV. It strives to appeal to all of the people some of the time.

Training opportunities, ITV companies

Individual ITV companies occasionally offer training schemes, some of which are for graduates. For further information, contact the ITV companies (and see p. 94).

The independent producers – who are they? what do they do?

Independent producers are not to be confused with the Independent Television companies. They are production companies which have been making corporate videos for many years. Some have been engaged in broadcast work for specific programmes, and so will be experts in particular fields. For example, a television company doing a news or current affairs article on the Stock Exchange may ask an independent producer who has had experience in this area to make the feature. This saves time and possible money. These producers are now competing for programme contracts with the BBC and ITV companies.

Cable and satellite stations

Cable and satellite stations will enlarge the choice of available television viewing channels. Although both appear to be gaining popularity, their impact on the industry has yet to be evaluated.

Cable television

Cable companies exist throughout the UK and are funded by subscriptions from households who are cabled into the network, and from advertising revenue. Cable television is transmitted from the cable station to the subscriber via the cable which is laid in the ground in the same way as the electricity supply. The cable station can offer a wide variety of programmes. Like the broadcast programmes, the sources of cable programmes can be wide. They can be either locally produced, bought from other countries (e.g., American soaps or game shows), or bought from satellite companies.

Satellite television

There are now ten satellites which are capable of transmitting 42 channels to countries in Europe. These range from low- and medium-power types to the new generation of high-power satellites, known as direct broadcast satellites (DBS). The signals from the low- and medium-power satellites require transmission stations to boost them. The signals are then relayed to individual households. The newer high-power satellite, however, allows individual households who purchase a rooftop satellite 'dish' not much larger than a dinner plate, and a black box converter, to receive satellite signals direct.

The competition of satellite companies to dominate at this early stage is now in evidence. The low- and medium-power satellite companies (Sky and very soon Astra), are already publicizing satellite TV, ahead of their high-powered rivals (BSB). The 'battlefield' will not only feature a variety of companies transmitting from different types of satellite. There already exist five different transmission standards. These are PAL, SECAM, B-MAC, C-MAC and D2-MAC. There are more to come and, unfortunately for the consumer, the systems are incompatible and will require different pieces of hardware. The choice of channels will increase, as will the opportunity for advertisers to reach wider audiences across Europe.

Key jobs in the television industry explained

Announcers

The announcer provides the link between programmes, introducing the next or future programmes. Much preparation goes on behind the scenes and the announcer must be able to work to deadlines and cope with the unexpected. Announcers need to have a wide knowledge of television programmes, be able to work unsocial hours and have good presentation skills.

Camera operator/trainee

The camera operator works in the studio and on outside broadcasts (OB), using electronic video cameras. Most programmes have rehearsals and members of the crew will run through the script checking the camera angles and shots. Each crew member has script notes outlining what is required. The camera operator wears headphones or 'cans' to receive instructions from the director in the production suite. In a studio between four and six cameras are used simultaneously and the production suite usually has six TV monitors displaying what each studio camera is viewing. The director then has to choose which shot to show and in which order.

New technology has reduced the size of cameras. This gives greater flexibility in shooting current affairs programmes and news stories where there is little time for rehearsal. These cameras, electronic news gathering (ENG) cameras or portable single unit (PSU) cameras, can easily be carried on the operator's shoulder.

Camera operators need a good technical understanding and an interest in photography or art. The job is demanding; hours are long and unsocial and co-operative team work is essential.

Design-related departments

Costume designer/assistant

The costume designer liaises with the production team on what is needed for the artist's wardrobe. A period drama, for example, would require the designer to do research so that even the smallest detail is historically correct. The costume department is responsible for dressing the actors and maintaining the costumes. Designers usually have art school, fashion or theatre training.

Graphic designer/assistant

The graphic designer creates titles, animated sequences and illustration, using both traditional skills and complex computer-aided design equipment. Liaison between different departments is essential to ensure that the graphics enhance the programme's overall feel. Graphic designers will usually have studied graphic design at a polytechnic or college.

Set designers/assistants

Set designers are responsible for interpreting the atmosphere and setting which the director, producer and writer have planned. The designer must understand the technical aspects of programme making as well as being skilled in theatre design and interior design. Historical programmes require research to ensure that the architecture and furniture are correct. Training at art or theatre school is required.

Make-up artist/trainee

The make-up artist makes actors, performers and singers fit their part. The work ranges from a simple 'dusting' over to avoid a shiny face on screen, to hairstyling and special effects like wounds and scars. The make-up artist must have tact and diplomacy. He or she is one of the last of the crew to see the actors or performers before they go in front of the camera. The main requirements for this job are beauty therapy, hairdressing or art school training. Amateur experience in the theatre is useful.

Director

The director needs a wide understanding of the job of every person involved in programme making. The director has to plan and make the programme, direct both the crew and the actors and ultimately oversee the work of the editor. The director's background experience must be wide and varied. He or she will generally have done a number of jobs in television prior to becoming a director.

Editor/assistant

Editing is the final stage in the making of a programme. The editor assembles the work in the way the director intended. Editors must be able to work in film and video, as many television programmes use both during a production. The editor needs the artistic ability to make creative decisions. The difference between film and video editing is in the equipment; film editing involves handling and physically cutting the film, whereas video editing is done on sophisticated keyboard equipment. Both require dexterity, an eye for detail and a lot of patience as well as the ability to work to deadlines (particularly when editing news information). Editors need a wide knowledge of production techniques and the ability to understand other people's ideas.

Engineers

Electronic engineers operate and maintain the complex communication equipment used in television. Their responsibilities include routeing of all cables, linking equipment, monitoring sound and picture signals and adjusting camera signals so that each picture is of the same quality in colour and clarity. Fault-finding and repair requires a high degree of technical understanding. Most engineers have studied electronic engineering or telecommunications to HND or degree standard. Engineers must work as part of a team and cope with shiftwork and irregular hours.

Floor manager/assistant

The floor manager is the go-between, linking the director and the people on the studio floor. The director keeps in two-way contact with the floor manager via headphones (the system referred to as 'talk-back'). The floor manager then relays the instructions to those on the studio floor. The floor manager has to advise the crew, actors and audience diplomatically to achieve the results the director wishes. Many floor managers would have started their career in the theatre, as assistant stage managers (ASM).

Journalists/reporters/correspondents

Journalists or reporters collect and write news items for news bulletins covering a wide variety of events and stories. Newswork is very demanding and unpredictable and journalists have to be ready to get to the story wherever it happens. Journalists must be very flexible, able to cope with pressure and meet deadlines. Some journalists work behind the scenes, writing for presenters, while others write and present the news themselves. Presenting requires a calm and professional manner because the programme goes out live.

Both the BBC and ITN have specialist correspondents who concentrate on particular topics, for example politics, finance, education and foreign affairs; some report from the countries they are covering.

Journalists, reporters and correspondents have generally had experience in local, regional or national newspapers, or on radio prior to joining television.

Librarians

Television companies have a vast reference collection. These libraries include music, sound effects, photographs, films and video tapes and programmes. All the material must be catalogued and stored. Nowadays many catalogues are computerized and the material is booked out and in as in a public lending library.

Lighting director

Lighting creates the right mood in a programme. The lighting director works closely with the production team and camera crew to create the best effect. He or she will be experienced, with a good knowledge of the equipment. Because much of the equipment is heavy and must be constantly moved around, the director has to be safety conscious. Lighting experience, perhaps electrician training in theatre or film, is essential.

Producer

In television the job of a producer often overlaps with the job of a director, and sometimes both are done by one person. The producer is the person who comes up with the concept for the programme. A producer is responsible for ensuring that the production is completed on time and within the budget. With the help of the production team, the producer must keep the production running smoothly. Many producers specialize in particular areas, for example light entertainment, current affairs or drama.

Production assistant

The production assistant (PA) provides administrative support, co-ordinates meetings, arranges rehearsals and notes any script changes prior to recording. While the programme is being recorded, the PA is usually seated beside the director in the production seat. The PA is responsible for cueing film and video tape inserts, cueing cameras and keeping accurate timing throughout. Typing and shorthand ability are essential as well as the ability to work under pressure for long periods.

Production manager

The production manager deals with the day-to-day organization connected with the programme and liaises with the director. The tasks are varied and include things like arranging accommodation and catering and dealing with last-minute hitches. To ensure the smooth

running of the programme, the production manager must be able to keep an eye on a number of aspects at once.

Researchers

Researchers work on a wide range of programmes. The researcher will be involved in a programme from the start and it is his or her job to contribute ideas and research background material to support the programme. The background material could be quite varied and may include providing contestants for a quiz programme, information on a guest for a chat show, or archive film. Most researchers are graduates and many have had media-related experience. It is a good idea to have some specialist knowledge.

Secretary/clerical staff

In every television company there are secretaries and clerical staff providing essential administrative back-up to the programme-makers as well as fulfilling the functions of administration, finance and legal departments as found in any large organization. Opportunities to progress do exist, but competition for advancement is fierce and many people can be disappointed if their sole aim in starting out as a secretary was to be promoted to other jobs in production. The job of a secretary is demanding; he or she must work to deadlines and cope with the unexpected. This needs experience and initiative. Good typing and shorthand skills are also important.

Sound technician/trainee

Sound technicians set up microphones on booms or stands, operate recording equipment and work under instruction from the sound supervisor who checks sound controls and levels. The sound supervisor has to have a lot of experience and it is his or her responsibility to mix and fade vocals, music or effects. Sound technicians must have excellent hearing and understand the technical aspects of sound recording. The job is demanding, the hours are long and unsocial and co-operative team work is essential.

Transmission controller (ITV companies)

Each ITV company has a transmission controller who checks the television company's output prior to transmission. The transmission controller is not involved in the actual making of any particular programmes. His or her job is to ensure the smooth flowing continuity of the television station's daily output of programmes. Programmes come from a variety of sources within ITV companies and it is the controller's job to monitor all the programmes, commercial breaks, and news bulletins, to ensure that the links between them are cued up on time. This is done at a presentation mixing console. The transmission controller checks the pictures being sent to the transmitter and the pictures which are broadcast from the transmitter to household television screens. A transmission controller must be able to anticipate potential problems and have quick reactions so that if problems do occur, he or she is able to respond quickly to ensure that the viewer doesn't receive a blank screen!

Vision mixer

The vision mixer's job is, in some ways, similar to that of the transmission controller in that he or she also works from a mixing console. However, unlike the transmission controller, the vision mixer works on the making of individual programmes.

The vision mixer sits in the production suite operating the vision control panel. The vision mixer can cut and fade pictures from each of the studio cameras and integrate pictures from other sources, for example video tape inserts, titles, etc. In front of the production suite is a bank of television monitors. Each displays a different picture. There is one monitor for each camera and others for inserts. The vision mixer assembles all these into an organized sequence.

Sales/marketing (ITV companies)

All the ITV companies rely on advertising revenue to fund the company, so sales and marketing departments are extremely important to any ITV company. Look at any paper which advertises jobs in the broadcasting industry and you will see that most of the jobs offered are in sales and marketing. This is because this is the fastest growing area of the business.

Sales and marketing staff liaise with advertising agencies, taking bookings for 'slots' in the commercial breaks. Much of the work is done over the 'phone with immediate input into a desk top computer. Sales staff have to be good negotiators and be able to calculate and quote competitive rates and possible percentage discounts quickly.

Marketing staff are involved in researching audience ratings and targeting of programmes. It is a demanding job as market research uses sophisticated methods of analysis to categorize the audience population according to what and when they watch and what they buy. This determines the types of products advertised at certain times of the day.

Profile

Graphics technician – Philip

Philip is a graphics technician in LWT (London Weekend Television)'s graphics department. He has been with the company for eighteen months, during which time he has been trained to assist the graphics design team, working largely as an Aston character generator operator.

At school Philip knew he wanted to do something in television, as camera work interested him. He had used VHS equipment at school and had been on a visit to a television studio; both experiences increased his enthusiasm for the industry. At school he took a good mix of subjects at O level – maths, English language, biology, physics, history, computer studies and art with a photography option. He then went on to study a BTEC National Diploma in audio-visual studies, which he chose because it would give him a good grounding in a variety of skills.

When he went to college Philip was one of the few students who had keyboard skills. He says it was an advantage to have a basic understanding of the keyboard when using video equipment. The course modules covered graphics, audio-visual, electronics, photography and computer studies. During his work experience in the industry he was placed in the AV department of a hospital, an educational company and a video facilities house. Course work projects, which included designing a board game and an AV presentation, counted towards the final exam grade. He also made a short tape slide presentation about his local area – past and present – incorporating old photographs as well as modern-day shots. Other work displayed at the final exhibition included posters, computer projects, electronics and a video.

Before he left college, Philip compiled a list of names and addresses of companies to contact with speculative applications. He applied to an advert for a junior graphics technician at LWT and was offered an interview. He took along well-presented examples of his course work, which gave him more confidence as he could provide the interview panel with a clearer idea of what he had covered on his course. The interview was successful.

Philip is one of three Aston operators. The Aston is an electronic character generator which has a variety of typefaces on disk, allowing the operator to enlarge the size, change colours or make other changes to the characters. When a selection is made, the graphics are stored for later broadcast. Philip was given full training on how to operate the Aston 3 and an overview of the making of a programme. LWT also sent him on a touch-typing course to improve his speed and accuracy.

The graphics department receives typed requisitions with all a programme's Aston requirements from the production assistant. Philip works with graphic designers, assisting them in making decisions about the typeface they will use for a programme's credits. The Aston allows the designer to see immediately how the graphics will look on screen. The Aston requirements have to be timed accurately so that they are in line with the programme music – Aston allows the credits to be rolled at various speeds as required.

The Aston is not only required at the beginning and end of each programme, but within the programme itself, as details may need to be displayed. For example, a sports programme may include a factfile on screen about a team or an individual's sporting performance.

After the programming has been completed, the disk is given to the production assistant; it is his or her responsibility to check all the details, including accurate spelling.

Philip is still in training and is learning how to operate the Aston 4 – a more sophisticated version of the equipment he uses daily. He is also involved in printing the information cards used on some game shows. When there is time, he makes master disks of all typefaces and catalogues them, as well as assisting others in his department. He is very happy in his present job and enjoys the variety of work and the environment.

5

Radio

Radio in Britain is dominated by the BBC's four national stations, BBC local radio stations and Independent Local Radio (ILR), often referred to as commercial radio.

Radio stations vary in their output, catering to different tastes. Some, like Radio 1 and many of the commercial stations, concentrate on contemporary music. Radio 4 and London Broadcasting Company (LBC) are mainly concerned with news and current affairs. Broadcasting time varies. Radio 2 and some commercial stations, for example, broadcast 24 hours a day. Radio stations also differ in size, depending on their budget. Many local radio stations are run on a 'shoestring' and welcome help from unpaid volunteers. Like all employment in media communications, job vacancies are scarce and competition is fierce.

In the White Paper on broadcasting the Government plans to introduce three commercial channels, and that there will be community radio. A new organization, to be called the Radio Authority, will regulate and oversee radio broadcasting.

BBC radio

The BBC controls Radios 1, 2, 3 and 4 as well as some 30 local radio stations. BBC radio, like BBC television, does not advertise and, similarly, is funded by the licence fees. Radios 1, 2, 3 and 4 are networked, which means that they are broadcast throughout the UK, and cover topics of national interest. BBC local radio stations are based in large towns, and broadcast to defined areas. They attempt to give their listeners a more personalized service, and therefore cover local issues as well as national stories, rather like local newspapers.

Independent Local Radio (ILR)

There are about 50 ILR stations throughout Britain and, like the BBC's local stations, they broadcast to their specific area. As their title suggests, they are independent and are funded by advertising revenue, and so have to compete with ITV, newspapers and magazines for advertisers. ILR is regulated by the IBA.

Each company handles its own staff recruitment and training. As many of these companies are small, they may not have adequate staff, time or flexibility to train new employees and often prefer to recruit experienced staff. Generally, local radio stations prefer local applicants.

The London Broadcasting Company (LBC) differs from other ILR

stations in that it specializes in providing a news and information service. The other commercial station in London, Capital Radio, concentrates on music. Independent Radio News (IRN) is a subsidiary of LBC and provides all ILR stations with news bulletins (rather like ITN providing news bulletins to ITV companies).

Community radio

Community radio in Britain is mainly located in metropolitan areas and it is estimated that there are approximately 500 of these stations broadcasting. Often they target specific groups of the listening public who feel inadequately served by the existing radio stations. In the mid-1980s a two-year experiment by the Government to look at the demand for community radio was cancelled. It is hoped future Government legislation will give licences and legalize the work of community radio stations.

Hospital radio

Most hospitals have a radio station which offers a service to their own patients. The station doesn't actually broadcast through the airwaves, but via wires to patients' headphones. Hospital radio has produced many successful people in main-stream radio companies. Valuable experience can be gained because, despite it being an amateur service, the programmes are polished and the newcomer can learn a great deal about programme content, technical operations and presentation.

Key jobs in the radio industry explained

Engineers/technical operators (TO)

The engineer and technical operator are responsible for the technical equipment involved in the production and transmission for radio. Work involves maintenance and the operating and setting up of equipment in some outside broadcasts (OB) – for example in the coverage of sporting events – and in the studio.

Journalists/reporters

The job of a journalist or reporter involves finding and reporting stories. This could be done either inside or outside the studio as it includes researching the background, interviewing people and then, back in the studio, editing and assembling the material into a newsworthy story. Deadlines are a constant pressure as most of the stories must be reported as soon after the event as possible. As a result, stories are often written on the spot. Apart from the obvious need for a flair for writing, the journalist has to be able to operate the technical equipment, including professional tape recorders and microphones, and to balance the sound for interviews. In addition, because the journalist may have to present the story personally, he or she must have a good broadcasting style. The working schedule is variable and shiftwork is common, demanding great stamina and commitment.

Music librarian

Radio companies have a vast collection of music on all formats (records, cassettes, reel-to-reel and compact disc), all of which have to be properly checked, stored and catalogued. Like a public lending library, all the music is indexed and classified. This enables any specified piece of material to be located easily. A wide knowledge of and interest in music is essential.

Music presenter

Being a music presenter or a disc jockey (DJ) has more to it than many newcomers realize. It is not just putting on records with a bit of chat in between. A lot of preparation is needed before the programme goes on air. The DJ chooses the records to be played from a play list which has to suit the programme's mood. The DJ also has to have a good idea of what he or she will be saying during the show. The DJ will also have to log all the records to be played (a legal requirement for royalty payments), and may also be involved in the preparation of other material such as jingles

or recorded interviews. During the broadcast, the DJ will need to be able to cue up, fade in, play and fade out the material (on record, tape, CD and, of course, the microphone). So good technical understanding, appreciation and ability are required. Timing is essential, as there are certain parts of the programme which have to be broadcast on time, like the news. The programme producer, for example, may signal that time is short and the news is due in one minute. The presenter will have to cut short the conversation (or music), to meet the deadline. Also, long periods of silence have to be avoided, because not only do they annoy the listener, but in commercial stations they waste valuable advertising time. The ability to think quickly and react correctly in any situation is important. The station's image also depends on the presenter and so the DJ has to be a good ambassador for the station.

News editor

The news editor has the final say on which stories will be used (and in what order) in news bulletins. Often this decision is taken only seconds before a news bulletin is due on air. The news editor will generally have worked as a journalist before becoming the editor.

Presenters

Presenters are usually experienced journalists. They do not just come into the radio station to read the news. They are involved in the writing and preparation of the news items that they will later present. They must be well read and well briefed on a wide variety of events and issues, and many start their working day by reading the major newspapers from Britain and abroad. They read the news on air and do links between programmes, which is referred to as 'anchoring'. It is essential that the presenter can stay calm and read flawlessly while coping with last-minute changes.

Producer

The producer conceives the programme idea and then puts the idea in motion. Budgets, scheduling and planning all have to be thought out and drawn up so as to convince others that it will be a worthwhile series or programme. The producer is also responsible for the management of the production team.

Programme assistant

The programme assistant works for the producer and has a variety of responsibilities. The work includes researching background information and organizing guest appearances as well as typing up information. The programme assistant may get involved in the technical aspects like checking cartridges (carts) and basic editing, especially if there are deadlines to be met and the pressure is on.

Programme secretary

The programme secretary provides the secretarial and administrative back-up for the programme. Often secretaries will aim to work on a programme whose content is of interest to them. Hours are irregular and, together with the necessity to keep to programme deadlines, work pressure may be high, so the ability to keep calm in a crisis is essential.

Sales/marketing

Commercial radio relies on advertising revenue. The more popular the station, the more it can charge for advertising time. The marketing staff, generally, have to maximize the station's audience listening figures. To do this they analyse the data which give them information about who listens to what station or programme and when. This gives them a good idea of the audience profile (age, sex, profession, etc.) for each programme and also what parts of the programme appeal to them. They are able to use this information to see what alterations can be made to the programmes to maximize audience figures. They then inform the advertisers what type and numbers of people listen at particular times. For example, they may find that many commuters listen early in the morning. This would therefore be an appropriate time for British Rail to advertise a new money-saving scheme for commuters.

Many staff are involved in co-ordinating the placement of commercials in the breaks. The sales staff negotiate these advertising slots, liaising with the agencies who buy the advertising slots and the companies who produce the actual commercials.

Sound operator

The sound operator is responsible for mixing and balancing the sounds to optimize the quality of the broadcast. This will include music from all sources and also sound effects and voices. Anyone who has to talk into a microphone on air, whether they be the presenter or a guest being interviewed, will be asked to do a sound check by saying something into the microphone so that their voice level can be checked and balanced. The operator works on a mixing desk, and so will need to have a sound understanding of the technical capacities of the equipment.

Station manager

The manager is responsible for setting up the studio to suit the needs of the programme, checking that equipment is operational and ensuring everything is ready for transmission. He or she has to be able to identify potential problems and deal with them when they can't be avoided. The station manager is responsible for ensuring tapes and discs are run at the right time and that the running order is adhered to. If there are other people involved, such as studio audiences, actors or guests, the manager must co-ordinate and brief them prior to the broadcast.

Profile

Production assistant – radio commercials – Debbie

Debbie currently works for a company which produces radio commercials for ILR stations throughout Britain. She has been in the job for two years, during which time she has gained valuable experience.

Before she worked in radio Debbie was all set to study sociology and psychology at university, but decided to take a year off to travel and think about her future. She had always been interested in a career in broadcasting and, while away, the question that kept going through her mind was that as she knew what she wanted to do, why should she delay it by going to university? Debbie admits to being impatient.

By the time she returned from her travels the decision was made and she began job hunting. She wrote to a number of companies highlighting her interest and enthusiasm, but despite getting interviews, she didn't find a job. Many companies advised her to learn to type, which she did and as a result she found work temping in a variety of organizations. Then a friend working in a film company told her about a junior runner vacancy. She went along and got the job where she spent a year as a runner delivering and collecting work and making tea. She did not see promotion coming so she decided to look for another job with more prospects. She saw an advertisement in the *Guardian* for a receptionist/secretary in a production company making commercials. The interview was more daunting than she had expected, with four directors in a studio full of equipment. She pretended to be confident, although she felt nervous, answered the questions as fully as possible and showed that she had a sense of humour. Debbie feels it is crucial not to be frightened to speak: 'How else will they find out about you?' This was her lucky break. She got the job and says that it was her experience as a runner in a film company which helped her to do this.

She had worked as a receptionist/secretary for three months when the next break came, when the production assistant left. Her managers could see she had potential, so she was promoted. Initially she was involved in tape copying, sending out the commercials to the ILR stations and learning the paperwork. There are a lot of legal requirements which must be satisfied before a commercial goes on air. The radio production company liaises with advertising agencies, their clients, actors' agents and the Independent Television Association (ITVA), the Association of Independent Radio Contractors (AIRC) and the Copy Clearance Secretariat.

The advertising agency, the name of the advertiser, the product, the length and title of the commercial, the recording date, the transmission area and date, the name of the voice-over artist and sound effect details must all be logged. For music copyright, the music source has to be identified so that royalties can be paid (if appropriate) via the Mechanical Copyright Protection Society (MCPS).

Before making a radio commercial, the company receives three different scripts from the advertising agency. Debbie's job is to read the script and give a quote on the cost of producing it. The company have a rate card which quotes the costs of studio time, tapes/cartridges (carts), sound effects, live band/library music, most of which are charged by the hour. If the quote is accepted, work begins. This demands meticulous preparation, arranging the actor for the voice-over, or more usually dealing with the actor's agent, booking the studio, preparing sound effects and getting the script cleared. Debbie finds her typing skills useful when liaising with all these people and organizations.

For a single 30–40-second commercial, the studio is booked for an hour. The actor will be in for approximately half that time. Debbie may have to give directions, asking for special emphasis in parts of the script; 'Most actors are used to doing commercials and voice-overs and know exactly what is expected,' she says. Prior to recording, she also makes or gathers sound effects, which can take a lot of time and energy. When all the sound is ready, the commercial is mixed together and edited so that the timing is exact. The eight-track recording is then transferred to ¼-inch tape which is then the transmission master. From this copies are made to send to the radio stations. If time is short and the commercial is due on air within the same week, the company will make up cartridges (carts) so that they can be played immediately by the radio station. One of Debbie's final tasks then is to notify the Performing Right Society (PRS) so that royalties can be paid.

Debbie finds her job demanding and varied. 'You have to be very organized, able to plan in advance, cope with deadlines and be accurate with time.' Her next step? She has made no precise plans but she is keen to see how television commercials are made and will perhaps move on to that.

BBC local radio reporter – Andy

Andy has just completed a year's intensive training as a BBC local radio trainee reporter and is now based with Radio WM in Birmingham.

At school, Andy had always thought that he would become an author. He had a romantic image of what being an author meant; i.e., growing a long white beard and sitting in coffee bars discussing projects with other learned friends.

At high school he studied languages and arts subjects and had no clear ideas about his career, although travel and politics interested him. Then his career ideas altered when he realized lawyers and diplomats generally earned a lot more money than writers. University was mentioned as a possibility and he went to a sixth form college and chose to study economics, French (to travel) and maths for A levels. He also studied Spanish at O level. Andy describes himself as a bit of a swot, but unlike others in his year, he never assumed he would go to university, as it would be something he would have to work hard for. However, his head teacher saw his potential and entered him for the Oxford University entrance exam. Much to his surprise he passed. His parents were delighted as no one else in the family had stayed on in education past sixteen.

He enrolled to study politics, economics and philosophy. He really enjoyed being at Oxford as it brought him into contact with lots of different types of people and broadened his outlook. He did not think about what he would do next until his final year. He was interested in Third World politics and economics and considered doing an MA in development studies. In his spare time he did some disc jockeying on a hospital radio, which he says was just for fun. It never occurred to him that it might be useful experience for his career.

After university he went to Africa to work as a volunteer on a short-term project for three months. While there he got dysentery and decided this type of work was not for him.

When Andy returned, he got a teaching job in Spain, through a friend, but soon realized that he did not want to spend the rest of his life teaching. The one thing he had enjoyed was working as a DJ. He tried to get a job on Spanish radio but only succeeded in getting unpaid work on different stations. He decided to try writing for radio, magazines or newspapers. After many rejections, he applied for some courses in radio journalism, including the BBC's local radio trainee reporter scheme. He did a lot of work to enhance skills he knew would be useful; he taught himself to type, he read widely, he studied two languages and translated when foreign guests came to radio stations (unpaid). All this voluntary work gave him a basic understanding of what was expected and eventually he was offered places on four courses, including one on the BBC's scheme, which he chose to accept.

Andy says his job in radio is fairly easy to describe: 'It's hectic, never dull. It's varied but never well paid.' He works in two main areas: programmes and news. In the first he spends most of his day preparing a couple of three-minute pieces for the breakfast show or the drive-time show. They can be serious, even controversial, or light and entertaining. They generally consist of packages of two or more interviews linked with his voice and enhanced with effects and music. For news the emphasis is on shorter, harder interviews and information packages. The two categories often coincide; both require similar journalistic skills – being able to 'sniff out' a good story and having the persistence to follow it through. Imagination and inventiveness are also very important.

'Above all, in radio you have to be able to work under pressure. Deadlines are short and unforgiving. The best way to find out what it's all about is by listening to a local station and maybe approaching the editor to see if you can spend a few days in the newsroom watching the reporters at work.'

Andy feels the BBC's local radio training scheme offers an unequalled route to a career in radio journalism. It gives you a chance to work on several stations as a trainee and gain experience as well as contacts, which are always useful when applying for jobs.

Andy says that if you are keen on getting into radio journalism you have to be persistent, applying for college courses and to newspapers, the ILR and the BBC – don't give up even when you receive rejections; the next application could be lucky.

6
Courses and practical training

This book has already emphasized the difficulty of getting that first break. Newcomers will encounter fierce competition and will need to maximize their opportunities. In applying for training or work, much depends on the performance at interview, the CV and the methods of approach. Before you can address the question of the interview and your CV, you must first have a firm idea of what area of work you are interested in. This will not only give an indication of what you will need in terms of relevant experience, but your commitment will show through at the interview. The advice to 'first find out what you want to do' sounds obvious, but nowadays it may not be enough to have only a 'rough idea', so before going through the arduous task of firing off millions of applications to prospective employers, it might be more efficient to research the options first.

There is no better way of building up a feel for the terrain than by getting some practical experience in it. One of the easiest ways of doing this is to get involved in a production. Amateur theatre groups and work-shops are a good place to start. Although not all the jobs outlined in previous chapters will be represented in amateur groups, the important ones still have to be done, although in smaller productions one person may be doing two or three different jobs. This experience will give you a good feel of what there is to be done and in what sequence. It will also help you to decide if the work is suited to your skills and abilities, and which particular areas you prefer.

Being part of a production may also give you valuable first-hand experience of the equipment. Alternatively, you can gain practical experience through developing hobbies such as photography, electronics, art, writing, etc. Getting involved prior to applying for courses, training and jobs will enable you to decide if this is the right choice for you, while giving you some useful preparation and background knowledge of your chosen field.

So now that you know what you want to do, the next thing is to examine what courses and training are available to help you on your way.

There are many places in the UK which offer relevant courses. These may be schools, colleges, art schools, universities, polytechnics, adult educational institutes, community workshops or art centres. Some courses follow a more theoretical approach to the subject, leading to formal qualifications recognized by the industry. Others adopt a more practical, 'hands on' approach, emphasizing involvement. Either way, courses are popular and entry is competitive, so commitment is essential.

There are a variety of courses to choose from and it would be wise to make sure that a particular course meets your needs and aspirations before applying. Other considerations include choosing between studying because you want a recognized qualification or studying for interest's sake alone, between full-time or part-time study, and between a formal syllabus or one with a workshop structure. The outcome of these decisions will depend on past experiences, current situations and job expectations.

Entry criteria for courses vary but what they all do have in common is that applicants are expected to be able to demonstrate an interest in broadcasting. Interests which are considered relevant include the creative arts, photography, super 8-mm film, video, theatre, radio, painting and writing. Technical skills considered relevant include electronics, sound engineering and computer technology.

Apart from courses at educational institutions, practical training opportunities exist operated by special training establishments. These provide training of a more practical nature.

Libraries, careers offices and adult education institutes provide sources of information on the availability and location of courses and practical training.

With rare exceptions, few organizations offer systematic training. Organizations which employ permanent staff tend to train them on the job. Occasionally a company may sponsor an employee to attend a short course at an educational establishment, to learn a specific skill. More often than not, it is left to individuals to organize this themselves.

The unions

The Association of Cinematograph, Television and Allied Technicians (ACTT) is the union which represents the technical, production and creative grades of work within independent television, independent radio, the film industry and some other related areas. Obtaining a union card is important and is gained by first securing an ACTT graded job which has been notified through the union's vacancy list. After approximately one year in the job, union membership is obtained by getting existing union members to support your application to join. Applications are processed by internal panels through the divisional membership committee and the General Council. Initially the union card will have certain restrictions. After two years those restrictions will be lifted.

The Broadcasting Entertainment Trades Alliance (BETA) covers staff in the BBC, theatre craft and general grades within film and video.

The other main broadcasting unions are the National Union of Journalists (NUJ) which also has a union card system, and the Electrical, Electronic, Telecommunications and Plumbing Union (EETPU).

ACTT workshop declaration

The workshop declaration is an agreement between the British Film Institute (BFI), Channel 4, the Regional Arts Associations, the Independent Film and Video Association and the Association of Cinematograph, Television and Allied Technicians (ACTT). Its aim is to ensure that workshops are properly funded and staffed to provide non-commercial and grant-aided film and video tape work. The declaration aims to help workshops to develop audiences, research, education and community work in the widest sense. Workshops are democratically controlled and profits are ploughed back into further workshop productions.

The workshop sector can be divided into two parts: franchised and non-franchised. Franchise workshops are generally established units which have done a considerable amount of work and gained credibility. To become franchised, a workshop has to apply to the ACTT and the other establishments mentioned above. Once it has become franchised it is eligible to have its work considered for broadcast by Channel 4. In addition, ACTT workshops are more likely to be offered work on commercial productions. Non-franchise workshops are those groups which endeavour to make the medium more accessible to their local community via training, equipment hire and production work, often covering local issues. Workshop addresses can be found in the *BFI Yearbook*.

Training courses

Joint Board for Film Industry Training (JOBFIT)

JOBFIT was set up in May 1985 by the ACTT, the British Film and Television Producers Association (BFTPA) and the Independent Programme Producers Association (IPPA). The Advertising Film and Video Producers Association (AFVPA) and Channel 4 are also sponsors of the scheme. Funding is derived from levies on productions throughout the industry.

JOBFIT is the first systematic, industry-wide training scheme in the freelance film-making sector and it trains new entrants up to junior film-technician grade. Trainees are attached to various film productions over a two-year training period. In addition, off-the-job training is provided at recognized film schools. Training is specifically in the technical and production grades of film making covered by the ACTT. These are art department assistant, clapper/loader, second assistant editor, assistant sound recorders, assistant script supervisor, assistant boom operator, third assistant director. JOBFIT is not designed to train producers, directors or scriptwriters.

During the first year, trainees on the scheme gain an insight into a wide range of skills to give them a thorough grounding in all aspects of the film industry. This enables the trainees to make decisions about the specialist area they would like to pursue in their second year. JOBFIT trainees are extra to the crew and are paid an allowance. On satisfactory completion of the two-year programme, trainees become eligible for ACTT membership in a junior grade of their chosen specialist area.

While no specific academic qualifications are required, successful JOBFIT trainees must have a demonstrable commitment and enthusiasm for films and film making, good communication skills, a strong visual sense, all-round literacy and manual dexterity. A willingness to travel, work long hours and live away from home are important considerations for potential trainees. The minimum age for entry onto the scheme is eighteen, however there is no upper age limit. JOBFIT is a national scheme and takes trainees from throughout the UK. It is committed to an equal opportunities policy and strongly encourages and supports applications from women and ethnic minorities.

For further information, contact

JOBFIT, 4th Floor, 5 Dean Street, London W1V 5RN.

Cyfle training scheme

Cyfle was set up in October 1985 by the ACTT in Wales, The Welsh channel Sianel Pedwar Cymru (S4C) and Teledwyr Annibynol Cymru

(TAC), the association of independent producers in Wales.

Cyfle is a two-year training aimed at Welsh-speaking people, or those who will endeavour to learn the language during the scheme. Applicants must show genuine enthusiasm for film and television and understand the demands of the industry. Trainees are allocated placements with various producers on a variety of productions and move from one department to another which enables them to gain a wide range of skills. In the second year they specialize and are given further attachments. Off-the-job training is also part of the scheme. Trainee attachments are supernumery, but Cyfle trainees are paid an allowance.

Applicants must be under 25 years of age and be able to show their genuine enthusiasm for and interest in the television industry. The ability to speak Welsh is essential, although applicants who will endeavour to learn the language during the scheme will be considered. Academic qualifications are not required for entry.

For further information, contact

Cyfle, Gronant, Penrallt Isaf, Caernarfon, Gwynedd LL55 1NW.

Scottish Film Training Trust

The Scottish Film Training Trust's Technician Training Scheme was set up in 1978. It is devoted to technical and creative training for Scotland's independent film and video industry. The Trust is financed by companies involved in film, the Scottish Film Council, the Scottish Arts Council and the EEC Social Fund.

The Technician Training Scheme recruits three people per year. Trainees undergo an intensive six-week induction course, followed by a series of individual attachments and visits to film laboratories, studios and facility houses. During the scheme, they also produce their own five–ten-minute film. These trainees receive student bursaries and, on successful completion of their course, become eligible for ACTT membership in the assistant grades.

Applicants must be Scottish and committed to working in Scotland. Genuine interest and long-term commitment to develop a career in the technical grades of the independent sector must be demonstrated. The target age range for the scheme is 20–30. The Trust particularly encourages women to apply. A full driving licence is essential.

For further information, contact

Scottish Film Training Trust (SFTT), Dowanhill, 74 Victoria Crescent Road, Glasgow G12 9JN.

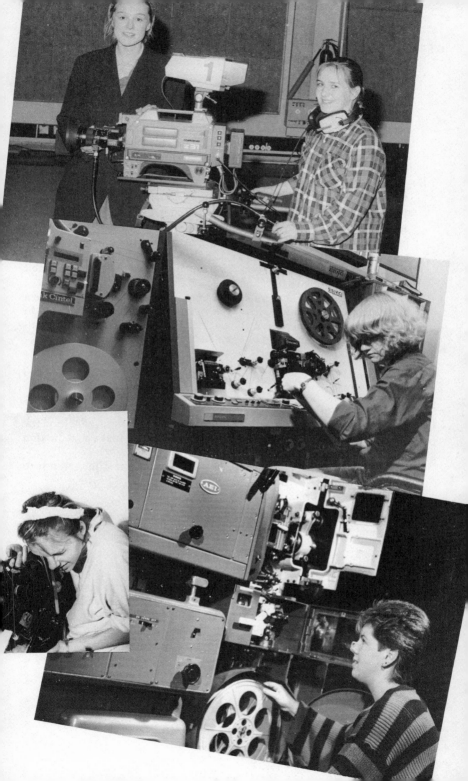

North East Media Training Centre (NEMTC)

The NEMTC was set up in 1986 by the North East Media Development Council. Its aim is to develop the media industry further within the north east of England and to train people for such jobs. The NEMTC is funded by the five local authorities in Tyne and Wear and two courses are available.

Two-year, full-time course

There are approximately 30 places on this course, the majority of which are given to Tyne and Wear residents. The first-year trainees gain a broad base of experience in film and video production. In the second year, they specialize in some particular area, e.g., production management, vision mixing, sound recording, etc. The scheme gives both practical and theoretical training in film and video. Trainees receive an allowance.

There is no stated academic requirement but applicants must have a genuine interest in film, video or television and, ideally, wish to work in the region on completion of the course. The NEMTC particularly encourages applications from women and ethnic minorities.

Twelve-week, pre-entrant training course in 16-mm film and low-band video

This course is aimed at people under 25. Training is full time and covers the full range of craft and organizational skills which are available on the two-year course. Trainees learn the skills required to make a production and produce a short film or video.

Applicants must be under 25 years of age with a genuine interest in film, video and television.

For further information, contact

North East Media Training Centre, Stonehills, Shields Road, Gateshead, Tyne and Wear NE10 0HW.

National Short Course Training Programme (NSCTP)

The NSCTP was set up in 1983 to offer an in-service retraining and updating course for freelancers working in the film and television industry. It is based at the National Film and Television School in Beaconsfield, Buckinghamshire and offers a wide range of courses lasting from three to ten days, aimed at technicians, performers and writers already employed in the industry, and other courses aimed at newcomers with a basic understanding.

For further information, contact

The National Short Course Training Programme, The National Film and Television School, Beaconsfield Studios, Station Road, Beaconsfield, Buckinghamshire HP9 1LG.

Other initiatives within the industry

From time to time the BBC, ITV companies and Channel 4 offer specific training courses. Check with the companies in your region to find out if they have plans to run any courses in the near future. The training is often for a limited period only and is aimed at specific groups such as the unemployed, women or people from ethnic minorities. This type of training does not always guarantee a job on completion of the course, but the experience and contacts will always be useful.

Profile

JOBFIT trainee, 1986–88 – Mark

Mark secured a place on the first intake of JOBFIT. This is his story so far.

Mark's school life was rather chequered. He felt he did not fit in because he questioned too much, and consequently his academic achievements were disappointing. He later picked up at college the qualifications which he did not get at sixteen. Various career ideas went through his mind: zoologist, lawyer, journalist . . . It was his interest in the latter which started the ball rolling. Together with a small group of friends he decided to publish a magazine aimed at young black people. The concept was ambitious and the group had to put a lot of energy into the project. *Black on Black Magazine* was written, organized and distributed by the group themselves, the print run being too small for a major distributor. The hardest aspect was trying to sell advertising space as advertisers wanted a publication with a large circulation before they were prepared to negotiate on prices and space in the magazine.

Increasingly, Mark became more interested in television. Then he met someone who was involved in producing Third World documentaries. This gave him the opportunity to watch how film is edited and how a production is put together. Throughout this stage, he had a series of jobs to support himself and his family. He was a dishwasher at a restaurant in the evening, which gave him time during the day to hustle and to make contacts. Later he worked issuing tickets in a car park. Between jobs, when he had saved enough money, he would study. This is how he financed himself through O and A levels, although, in the end, he did not complete his A levels because he felt that he was only taking them to please other people rather than for his own interest. He then went to the National Short Course Training Programme (NSCTP) and did a course in production management. Here he was able to meet people who were good contacts and capable of offering him good advice.

Mark feels his first real break came when he secured a job at Thames Television, cataloguing films and video tapes in the vast library there. The job of the librarian is clerical but requires initiative and good organizational skills. He remembers instances when programmes would require pictures and he would be given little time to find them. Then the pressure was on to produce the various bits of material by the deadline. Working long hours and being paid overtime enabled him to be more financially secure. He put spare money away to finance other courses and plans for his future. The job at Thames also enabled him to meet editors and to watch and learn more about their skills. These experiences made him more confident about which career he wanted to pursue.

Mark heard about JOBFIT through an advertisement in *The Voice* and through the *Guardian's* media pages and realized that it would give him the training and opportunity he wanted, so he applied for a place. However, before applying he found out as much as he could about the scheme and thought carefully about the application form. Then he took his time filling it in making sure he outlined all his experience so far and highlighted his commitment. Mark says he is often asked what he considers the deciding factor in him being offered a place on the JOBFIT scheme. The answer is commitment.

During the two interviews for JOBFIT, he felt positive and happy about his interview technique. When the letter arrived telling him of his acceptance, it was the break he wanted; an introduction to the film industry. However, he did not take up his place until he had completed his contract with Thames, as he was determined to see that through.

His JOBFIT group, Group 2, started their training with a six-week induction course at the National Film School. Mark felt this induction period was essential as it gave trainees the opportunity to learn the basics and the jargon before they were attached to a production. Mark joined JOBFIT with the desire to learn as much as he could about the industry and then to go on to become an editor eventually. However, attachments to productions and courses changed his aspirations and he began specializing in sound.

Mark's first attachment was to a major feature film which enabled him to learn, at first hand, the rigours of the industry. He was placed in the editing department and was involved in rubber-edge numbering (numbering the edge of film) the complete film, which is a lengthy job, requiring a lot of patience. Later attachments included working on commercials and features in the sound department. He felt his knowledge of editing made him appreciate the importance of keeping accurate logs of the sound track and how well-prepared sound sheets will assist the editor in the cutting room.

JOBFIT is not an easy option and training is intensive, both on attachments and in school. It is comprehensive and the practical and theoretical training complement each other. Hours are long as trainees are expected to work the same hours as the rest of the crew. It is important that you are quick to learn, as on attachment no one has the time to stop and show you how something is done if you did not understand it first time.

Mark completed his two years with JOBFIT in March 1988, and his training has now made him feel confident about his future. He has since secured work as a sound assistant, working freelance. JOBFIT also enabled him to gain experience and make contacts, which he hopes will be useful in the future.

Profile

Film degree student – Jillian

Jillian is currently studying for a BA (Hons) in film and video. Her interest in film and television started while she was at secondary school when, as a contestant on a television quiz for school pupils, she watched the making of a programme. In the sixth form she studied history, English literature and art A levels and film studies O level, which was a new subject at her school, taught by a history teacher who was very enthusiastic about film. She also did a short course in film which helped to focus her interest more specifically. As the course was practical, she was able to gain hands-on experience and through this she became interested in editing.

After A levels she decided to get a job in the industry for a year prior to going on to study film, and she soon got a job as a runner in a post-production film company. Jillian said it helped to know the central London area well, as from day one she was sent out to collect and deliver films from and to other companies or clients. Days were long, beginning in the morning with getting croissants and coffee for the staff's breakfast, then on to hand-delivering mail. During lunchtime she was on switchboard cover, operating telephones. Other duties included sending films off to processing labs, more delivery work, buying newspapers and anything else that was needed.

After gaining some initial experience of the industry, she progressed to edge-numbering (also called rubber numbering). This means numbering the film along its edge prior to editing. It's a lengthy task, but has to be done. Jillian was also involved in syncing-up film. This involves matching up the frame of film with the clapperboard on it to the sound of the clapperboard snap on the soundtrack. Doing these jobs gave Jillian greater confidence, and she lost her fear of the industry as she grew to understand it. It also enabled her to make contacts and gave her a solid foundation of basic skills.

During her stint as a runner she applied for a degree in film. Her interview went well, as she could relate many of the questions to her work, and she secured a place on the three-year course, starting September 1987. This was an opportunity to learn more about film and develop her creative skills, as the course links the practical to the theoretical. The course covers all areas of film making, from the initial ideas for a production, planning the script, and making a storyboard, to filming on location, organizing lighting, camera, and sound equipment, and finally on to editing and sound dubbing.

Having completed her first year, Jillian is still keen on editing and feels confident that when she graduates she will have good skills to offer. Ultimately, her ambition is to become a director, but she is very aware that this goal is a long way off. In the meantime she would like to become more involved in acting workshops, to gain a better understanding about actors and their work.

Summary of qualifications

The following list is meant only as a guide. The list of course centres under some of the qualifications is not comprehensive, but gives a general outline of the range of courses available. Consult course directories in your careers office for more information.

City and Guilds of London Institute (CGLI)

These are mainly skill-based examinations. The range of subjects is wide and academic content varies depending upon the subject. City and Guilds courses are normally available at colleges of further education and may be studied part time.

Technical and Vocational Education Initiative (TVEI)

These are four-year courses in schools and colleges for fourteen to eighteen-year-olds. TVEI aims to make the curriculum more practical and relevant to the world of work. TVEI programmes follow a pattern of core subjects with relevant options. GCSE and A levels are taken.

Certificate of Pre-vocational Education (CPVE)

A one-year course for sixteen-year-olds, providing a link between education and the world of work. The vocational studies include business studies, technical studies, production, distribution or service to people. The course includes three weeks' work experience.

General Certificate of Secondary Education (GCSE)

The GCSE is a new unified system of examinations which has replaced GCE O levels and CSEs. It aims to achieve a balance between knowledge, understanding and skills. Assessment is by course work and final examination.

BTEC/SCOTVEC National Diploma and Certificate

Entry generally requires four GCSE passes or a BTEC First Certificate. The length of study is two years. Many courses have work-experience modules.

Colleges offering BTEC National Diploma – Design (audio-visual):

Brunel Technical College
Ashley Down, Bristol BS7 9BU.

Central Manchester College
East Manchester Centre, Taylor Street, Gorton, Manchester M18 8DG.

Dewsbury College, School of Art and Design
Cambridge Street, Batley, West Yorkshire WF18 5BJ.

Epsom School of Art and Design
Ashley Road, Epsom, Surrey KT18 5BE.

Harrogate College of Art and Technology
Hornbeam Park, Hookstone Road, Harrogate, North Yorkshire
HG2 8QT.

Kidderminster College of Further Education
Hoo Road, Kidderminster, Worcestershire DY10 1LX.

Longlands College of Further Education
Douglas Street, Middlesbrough, Cleveland TS4 2JW.

Sandwell College of Further & Higher Education
Wednesbury Campus, Woden Road South, Wednesbury, West Midlands
WS10 0PE.

South Thames College
Department of Design and Media, Wandsworth High Street,
London SW18 2PP.

*Colleges offering BTEC National Diploma – Design communications
(media studies)*

Kingsway College
Hugh Myddleton Building, Sans Walk, London EC1.

Lowestoft College
St Peter's Street, Lowestoft, Suffolk NR3.

BTEC/SCOTVEC Higher National Certificate and Diploma

Entry generally requires five GCSE passes, one at A level, or a BTEC
National Diploma or Certificate in an appropriate subject. The length of
study is two years. Many courses have work-experience modules.

*Colleges offering BTEC Higher National Diploma – Design (communi-
cations):*

Bournemouth & Poole College of Art & Design
School of Photography Film & Television, Wallisdown Road, Poole,
Dorset BH12 5HH.
(Film and television)

Dewsbury College, School of Art & Design
Cambridge Street, Batley, West Yorkshire WF17 5JB.
(Audio and television)

Gwent College of Higher Education
Faculty of Art & Design, Clarence Place, Newport, Gwent NPT 0UW.

Ravensbourne College of Design & Communication
School of Television and Broadcasting, Wharton Road, Bromley,
Kent BR1 3LE.
(Television programme operations)
(Television studio systems engineering)

Colleges offering BTEC Higher National Diploma theatrical studies:

London College of Fashion (The London Institute)
20 John Princes Street, London W1.
(Specialist make-up options)

Degree courses (undergraduate degree courses)

Entry generally requires five GCSE passes, two at A level. The length of
study is three to four years. Some courses are practical, others are more
theoretical.

Colleges offering degree courses

Derbyshire College of Higher Education
Kedleston Road, Derby DE3 1GB.
(BA Hons photographic studies)

Dorset Institute of Higher Education,
Wallisdown Road, Wallisdown, Poole BH12 5HH.
(BA Hons communication and media production)

Harrow College of Higher Education
Watford Road, Norwick Park, Harrow, Middlesex HA1 3TP.
(BA Hons photography, film and video)

King Alfred's College
Sparkford Road, Winchester, Hampshire SO22 4NR.
(BA Hons drama [theatre and television studies])

London College of Printing (The London Institute)
Elephant & Castle, London SE1 6SB.
(BA Hons film, video)

Manchester Polytechnic
Capital Building, School Lane, Didsbury, Manchester M20 0HT.
(BA Hons design for communication media)

Newcastle-upon-Tyne Polytechnic
Faculty of Art & Design, Squires Building, Sandyford Road,
Newcastle upon Tyne NE1 8ST.
(BA Hons media production)

West Surrey College of Art & Design
Falkner Road, The Hart, Farnham, Surrey GU9 7DS.
(BA Hons photography, film and video, animation)

Postgraduate courses

Entry generally requires an undergraduate degree or the equivalent. The
length of study is variable.

Colleges offering postgraduate courses in film/television

University of Bristol
Department of Drama, 29 Park Road, Bristol BS1 5LT.
(Certificate in radio, film & television – 1 year)

London International Film School
24 Shelton Street, London WC2H 9HP.
(Diploma in film making – 1 year)

National Film and Television School
Beaconsfield Studios, Station Road, Beaconsfield,
Buckinghamshire HP9 1LG.
(Associateship – 3 years)

Royal College of Art
Kensington Gore, London SW7 2EU.
Department of Film and Television
(MA (RCA) film making – 2 years)
Department of Animation
(MA in animation – 2 years)

Colleges offering postgraduate courses in radio journalism:

City University
Graduate Centre for Journalism, 223–227 St John Street,
London EC1V 0HB.
(Diploma in radio journalism – 1 year)

London College of Printing
Elephant & Castle, London SE1 6SB.
(Post-graduate diploma in radio journalism – 1 year)

Polytechnic of Central London
School of Communications, 18–22 Riding House Street,
London W1P 7PD.
(Certificate in radio journalism – 1 year)
This course is specifically for ethnic minorities.

Lancashire Polytechnic
Fylde Street, Preston PR1 7DP.
(Post-graduate radio and television course – 1 year)

University College, Cardiff
Centre for Journalism Studies, 34 Cathedral Road,
Cardiff CF1 9YG.
(Post-graduate diploma in journalism studies – 1 year)

7

Practical steps

Entry paths

Generally, people entering the industry start in junior or trainee positions. This is true whatever your qualifications, as there is still a lot to learn about the work of the organization and how to put your skills into practice. What most employers are looking for in the selection process is common sense, enthusiasm and potential. Progression to more important technical positions can take time, not only because the acquisition of specific skills takes time, but also because a vacancy has to exist before you can be promoted into it.

Employers are keen on candidates who can demonstrate experience in the use of basic equipment, practical involvement with amateur groups and qualities which indicate ability and determination.

Applicants with vocational course experience should focus attention on companies operating in specific fields, using contacts made through course work-experience modules.

Points to remember when making job applications

- The majority of newcomers to the industry start at the bottom. Progression within companies depends on a good track record.

- Technical jobs in the industry often demand certain qualifications, maths and physics being the two most commonly required.

- Creative jobs frequently require specific training, for example at art school. Without these relevant skills, it is harder for the job seeker to be successful.

- As stated previously, many of the jobs open to newcomers are in junior posts. At this level, wages in the industry are often low and for this reason companies frequently choose to employ young people still living in the family home. Older candidates can, however, impress employers with a broader range of experience and with their maturity. Be prepared to negotiate on a salary, know exactly what your expenditure outgoings are and how much you need to live on. Be realistic!

Curriculum Vitae
(CV or personal history sheet)

With the exception of television companies and larger organizations within broadcasting, few companies have their own application form. A newspaper advertisement of a vacancy will often require a letter of application and a CV. When making speculative applications, a CV is essential. Basically a CV contains all the facts that would be needed in a standard application form: name, address, telephone number, educational qualifications and employment details. Planning and designing the layout is necessary in order that all details are clear and, one hopes, impressive. Remember, a CV gives the employer his or her first impression of you, so headings should be clear and information concise, and do make sure it looks appealing. Do not forget to mention if you hold a full or provisional driving licence. Typing or keyboard skills can also be an asset.

A possible layout could be:

CURRICULUM VITAE

Personal information:	name, address, telephone number, date of birth
Educational details:	name and address of schools attended from eleven upwards, dates attended, exams taken – subject, date and result;
	name and address of colleges attended, dates attended, exams taken – subject, date and result.
Work experience:	include full-time and part-time employment, school/college work experience, dates of employment. For each, give a concise description of duties and relevant responsibilities.
	(If you have had experience within broadcasting, list the equipment you are proficient with. This will give the employer a measure of your skills.)
Interests/Hobbies:	include relevant interests or hobbies related to broadcasting, also other pursuits such as sport. Be careful that the list does not get too long.

Remember to keep your CV up to date!

Speculative applications

Job seekers often choose to blitz organizations, sending out over 100 letters at a time. Although this does display enthusiasm, it is costly and disappointing when few replies are returned.

Another approach is to select only a few, say, approximately fifteen organizations. Try to find out what work the company has been involved in, what equipment and resources it has, in other words, do some research. Then look at your CV and accompanying letter. Is it targeting the right employer? Do you need to adapt your CV? Try to put yourself in the employer's shoes. Would this CV prompt you to ask the applicant for an interview? If not, try to change the parts where you, as an employer, would like to see more or different information. Do not assume you can get away with one standard format; you may need two or three to suit the differing needs of the jobs you are enquiring about.

In such a fragmented industry, with so many small companies, who do you address your letter to when making speculative applications? Some larger organizations have a personnel manager, but in the majority of small companies the managing director will be in charge of recruitment, so address it to the top. The letter will be passed on if he or she is not involved in recruitment.

Speculative applications can be posted or taken to the company personally, depending on how close you live. If you do call in with your CV, enquiring about vacancies, do not expect the person in charge of recruitment to be able to see you. Ask the person on reception if you can leave your CV for whoever deals with new recruits and try to find out that person's name. It is very important to keep records of all your applications: the companies' names and addresses, the date you called in (or date you mailed the letter), and the person in charge of recruitment.

Approximately one week later, telephone the company. Plan in advance what you are going to say and adopt a business-like manner. Remember that he or she is a busy person, so do not waffle. Your 'phone call could be along these lines. 'Hello, I was given your name as being the person in charge of recruitment. I called in last Wednesday and left my CV for your attention. I am interested in a job as a runner or junior. I have had some experience via . . .'.

Impress them with your enthusiasm and remember to give them your name and telephone number. Work may not be available now, but often an organization will hold names in the event of needing a person at short notice. If an appointment is possible, you may only have a short time to impress the employer with your skills and enthusiasm and the reasons why he or she should be interested, so consider your delivery with care.

Job vacancies

As vacancies are scarce, advertised jobs must be responded to quickly. Vacancies in the trade or national press attract large responses. Libraries provide a good range of local and national newspapers and trade journals may also be available here.

The advert will state the method of application – by letter and CV, or by telephone. Some may specify a closing date for the application. Where the advert doesn't specify a closing date, try to apply as soon as you can because this shows enthusiasm.

Applying for jobs

By letter

Draft out a letter, not forgetting to mention what job you are applying for (the company may have several different job vacancies). If the advert has a reference number, quote this in your letter. Mention where you saw the advert and briefly state why you are interested and suitable for the post. Write (very clearly) or type the letter on A4 plain writing paper. It should be no more than one side long. Your CV has all your details, so there is no need to duplicate all this information in the letter. Keep a copy of the letter.

By telephone

Plan in advance what you are going to say and make a few notes to remind yourself. If you have to use a public telephone, choose one in a quiet place and make sure you have enough money. When 'phoning, have a pen and paper ready to take down any information the company will give you: the date and time of your interview, the address and name of the person you will see, any additional documents or work they want you to bring along, etc.

By application form

Fill out the application form in pencil; this will allow you to check that your information fits the allotted space. Check that all the information is correct and there are no spelling mistakes. When you are satisfied, fill it out in ink (black is the best colour because it photocopies clearly; blue photocopies badly). There is usually a space on the application form which asks for further details of your career, activities and the personal interests which you think are relevant to your application. Think carefully – do not just make a list of all the sports you do. Consider which hobbies and interests have given you relevant experience for the job you are applying for. Construct the information into paragraphs covering the key points. You do not have to go into every detail; if it is interesting you will be asked to expand the information at the interview. Remember, when applying for a job, the application form or letter and CV form the first impression the company will have of you and it is on this that you will be judged, so it is worth taking time to make sure your application is eye catching, informative, legible and interesting. With luck, it will secure you an interview.

Interviews

Before the interview

It doesn't matter whether the interview is for a job vacancy or a place on a course – the preparation is the same. Gather as much information as possible in advance about the company/college, the work/course, etc., familiarize yourself with key facts and possible questions and keep up to date by reading the media section in national newspapers and trade publications.

Job interviews

The majority of companies are not household names, so gaining information can be difficult. In the job advert, there will usually be a line or two about the type of work the company does and maybe the type of equipment they have. Small companies often have a brief publicity card, larger ones may have booklets. So when you contact the company in reply to the job advert, ask if they can send any information that might be helpful. Even if all they send is a rate card, it will still identify the type of equipment they have. Also consult reference books.

Television companies and larger facility companies are easier to research. The BBC and ITV companies produce information, they publish annual year books and you can also do the easiest research of all – watch television. At the end, when they roll the credits, see which company made the programme. This is particularly important when viewing Channel 4 as this company commissions programmes. The production company could be the one you are applying to.

Major facility companies frequently have glossy brochures, so 'phone them up and ask for information.

Applying for courses ...

Colleges all produce prospectuses, so compare different courses and familiarize yourself with course modules and what qualifications each course offers. Many colleges have open days when you can find out a lot more than is told in the prospectus: facilities, how many places, how many applications for those places, what past students have done after qualifying – this will give you a good indication of whether it is the right course for your needs.

Applications for full-time courses have deadlines and as they may go through clearing house systems, make sure you know the closing dates.

Preparation for course interviews is much the same as for jobs. You must do your research on the course and think what the possible questions might be. Be prepared to demonstrate enthusiasm, interest and commitment.

The interview day arrives . . .

Interviews are stressful for most people, even for the person who will be interviewing you! Prepare for the day; decide what you are going to wear the night before so there isn't a last-minute panic. In an industry where employees often dress casually, most employers will still expect more formal wear at the interview. The impression created when you first enter is important, as it may be the one they remember when you leave. Be confident, be calm and, most important of all, be yourself.

Consider taking well-presented examples of your work – photographs or an amateur film or video. VHS format is the most acceptable, so if you have a film, try to get it transferred to VHS video. Before you take a piece of work along, ask yourself a few questions. Is the work good? Are you proud of it? Do not take examples if they are not impressive.

During the interview, listen to questions carefully and ask for clarification if necessary. When answering questions, consider your reply and, if appropriate, try to relate your hobbies or previous work experience to the question and the industry.

At the end of the interview, when asked, 'Are there any more questions you want to ask?', think clearly. Often people ask a question because they feel it is obligatory . . . it is not!

Interview follow-up

If you are unsuccessful, consider writing or 'phoning the company to get feedback on your interview performance. Try to find out what let you down so that you can work on that. Let's hope it will not be a problem next time. Do not get disheartened if you are unsuccessful. As mentioned earlier, competition is always fierce. Remember, there will always be other opportunities, so try to learn from each interview to improve your performance, ready for the next.

The job seeker's checklist – what to do next...

- Find out as much as you can about jobs within the industry – reading this book will already have given you a good start.

- Get involved ... join a club or organization and get experience of practical work. Does your school or college have a photography club, a film society, a video unit, a computer club? If not, why don't you see if anyone else is interested and then start one up.

- Check what courses are offered locally, either on a part-time or a full-time basis. Get information from your careers office, adult education institute or reference library.

- Consult *Yellow Pages* to find out the names and addresses of companies involved in film, video, television and radio in your area. You have to be thorough because they can be listed under a number of different headings.

- Hospital radio – if you live in a large town or city, check to see if your hospital has its own radio station. These stations are run by unpaid volunteers. It is hard work but is a good opportunity to gain valuable experience.

- Television and radio programmes often issue free tickets for studio audiences. Write to your nearest BBC regional centre or ITV company audience ticket unit requesting information about how you can be invited. It is a good way to see how a programme is made.

- Two excellent museums to visit are:
  The National Museum of Film, Photography and Television
  Prince's View, Bradford, West Yorkshire BD5 0TR.
  The Museum of the Moving Image
  BFI South Bank, South Bank, London SE1 8XT.

- Contact organizations for more information. See Chapter 8 for names and addresses of useful contacts.

- Read as much as you can around the subject. Keep your eyes and ears open!

8
Further information

For a general guide to courses in practical training and theoretical studies in all aspects of TV, film and video, see the BFI's publications.

Information and vacancy sources

For further information and job vacancies there are a number of journals available:

Audio Visual   (monthly magazine)
Broadcast   (weekly magazine)
Guardian   (media pages – Mondays) (national daily newspaper)
Independent Media   (monthly magazine)
The Listener   (weekly magazine)
The Producer   (quarterly periodical – Association of Independent Producers)
Screen International   (weekly magazine)
Sight and Sound   (quarterly periodical – BFI)
Stage and Television Today   (weekly paper)
Televisual   (monthly magazine)
UK Press Gazette   (weekly magazine)

Reference books

AIP Independent Producers Handbook
Association of Independent Producers, 17 Great Pulteney Street, London W1R 3DG.

Audio Visual Directory
PO Box 109, Maclaren House, Scarbrook Road, Croydon, Surrey CR1 1QH.

BBC Annual Report and Handbook
BBC Publications, 35 Marylebone High Street, London W1 (published annually). Essential reading when applying to the BBC for a vacancy.

BFI Film and Television Yearbook
BFI, 21 Stephen Street, London W1P 1PL (published annually).
A lot of information about film and television, addresses of companies.

Contacts
The Spotlight, 42–43 Cranbourn Street, London WC2
(published annually). Stage, television and radio addresses.

Directory of Women Working in Film, TV and Video
WFTVN, 79 Wardour Street, London W1.

Film Bang 88 – The Scottish Film and Video Directory
Scottish Film Council, 74 Victoria Crescent Road, Dowanhill,
Glasgow G12 9JN.

Home Office, *Broadcasting in the '90s: Competition, Choice and
Quality*
HMSO, November 1988.

IBA Television and Radio
Independent Broadcasting Authority, 70 Brompton Road, London SW3
(published annually). Information about independent television and
radio companies. Essential reading when applying to ITV/ILR companies for a vacancy.

Kemps International Film and TV Yearbook
Kemps Group Limited, Bath Street, London EC1 (published annually).

Careers information from television companies

BBC Corporate Recruitment Services
Broadcasting House, London W1A 1AA. Write in for information about
non-engineering jobs in the BBC.

BBC Engineering and Technical Operations Recruitment
Broadcasting House, London W1A 1AA. Write in for information about
engineering and technical jobs.

Careers in Independent Television published by Hodder & Stoughton.

Useful addresses:

Advertising Film & Videotape Producers Association (AFVPA)
26 Noel Street, London W1V 3RD

Association of Independent Producers (AIP)
17 Great Pulteney Street, London W1R 3DG

Association of Independent Radio Contractors (AIRC)
Regina House, 259–269 Old Marylebone Road, London NW1

British Film Institute (BFI)
21 Stephen Street, London W1P 1PL

British Film & Television Producers Association (BFTPA)
Paramount House, 162 Wardour Street, London W1V 4LA

British Kine Sound and Television Society (BKSTS)
547–549 Victoria House, Vernon Place, London WC1B 4DJ

Business and Technician Education Council (BTEC)
Centre House, Upper Woburn Place, London WC1A 0HH

Cable Television Association (CTA)
295 Regent Street, London W1R 7YA

City and Guilds of London Institute (CGLI)
76 Portland Place, London W1N 4AA

Council for National Academic Awards (CNAA)
344–354 Grays Inn Road, London WC1X 8BP

Cyfle
Gronant, Penrallt Isaf, Caernarfon, Gwynedd LL55 1NW

Independent Broadcasting Authority (IBA)
70 Brompton Road, London SW3 1EY

Independent Film, Video and Photography Association (IFVPA)
79 Wardour Street, London W1V 3PH

Independent Programme Producers Association (IPPA)
58–51 Berwick Street, London W1V 4RD

Independent Television Association (ITVA)
Knighton House, 56 Mortimer Street, London W1N 8AN

International Visual Communications Association (IVCA)
102 Great Russell Street, London WC1E 3LN

Joint Advisory Committee for Radio Journalism Training (JACRJT)
46 Southway, Hampstead, London NW3

Joint Board for Film Industry Training (JOBFIT)
4th Floor, 5 Dean Street, London W1V 5RN

National Council for the Training of Journalists (NCTJ)
Carlton House, Hemnall Street, Epping, Essex CM16

The Newspaper Society
Whitefriars House, 6 Carmelite Street, London EC4Y 0JE

North East Media Development Council (NEMDC)
Norden House, 41 Stowell Street, Newcastle upon Tyne NE1 4YB

Royal Television Society (RTS)
Tavistock House East, Tavistock Square, London WC1

Scottish Film Training Trust (SFTT)
Dowanhill, 74 Victoria Crescent Road, Glasgow G12 9JN

Scottish Vocational Education Council (SCOTVEC)
38 Queen Street, Glasgow G1 3DY

Society for Education in Film and TV (SEFT)
29 Old Compton Street, London W1V 5PL

Women's Film, Television & Video Network (WFTVN)
79 Wardour Street, London W1V 3PH

Broadcasting unions

Association of Cinematograph Television & Allied Technicians
(ACTT)
111 Wardour Street, London W1V 4AY

British Entertainment & Trades Alliance (BETA)
181–185 Wardour Street, London W1V 4LA

Electrical Electronic Telecommunication & Plumbing Union (EETPU)
5–7 Clarendon Road, Luton, Bedfordshire LU2 7PU.

National Union of Journalists (NUJ)
314 Grays Inn Road, London WC1X 8DP.

Acknowledgements

The author and publishers thank the following for permission to
reproduce illustrations:

Pankino Productions Limited 10, 28
Royal College of Art 11 (top), 66, 72
The Services Sound and Vision Corporation, photographer
    Andrew Ward 11, 29, 30, 33, 49, 51, 58 (middle), 72, 73
Astra and GEC Aerospace 14, 44
Health Education Authority 17
'Conny Templeman', Umbrella Films Ltd 21 (top)
Frontroom Productions 21
The BBC 31
Southern Photographic Studios 36
The IBA 41, 56
International Television News 49
Capital Radio 55, 58 (top), 59
LBC 58 (bottom left, and right)
Central London Polytechnic 73 (top), 75, 79
'Paschali's Island', Virgin Vision 92